Network Solutions is either a registered trademark or trademark of Network Solutions, LLC in the United States and/or other countries.

Norton and Norton Internet Security are trademarks or registered trademarks of Symantec Corporation or its affiliates in the U.S. and other countries.

Novell and GroupWise are either registered trademarks or trademarks of Novell, Inc. in the United States and/or other countries.

OpenOffice.org is either a registered trademark or trademark of Team OpenOffice.org e.V. in the United States and/or other countries.

PayPal is either a registered trademark or trademark of PayPal, Inc. in the United States and/or other countries.

Pegasus Mail is either a registered trademark or trademark of David Harris in the United States and/or other countries.

Register.com is either a registered trademark or trademark of Register.com, Inc. in the United States and/or other countries.

Spybot is either a registered trademark or trademark of Safer-Networking Ltd. in the United States and/or other countries.

Streamload and MediaMax are either registered trademarks or trademarks of Streamload, Inc. in the United States and/or other countries.

Sun Microsystems, JavaScript, and StarOffice are either registered trademarks or trademarks of Sun Microsystems, Inc. in the United States and/or other countries.

Sunbelt Software and Sunbelt Kerio Personal Firewall are either registered trademarks or trademarks of Sunbelt Software Distribution, Inc. in the United States and/or other countries.

Sygate is either a registered trademark or trademark of Sygate Technologies, Inc in the United States and/or other countries.

ThinkFree is either a registered trademark or trademark of ThinkFree.com Corporation in the United States and/or other countries.

Trend Micro, HouseCall, and PC-cillin are either registered trademarks or trademarks of Trend Micro Incorporated in the United States and/or other countries.

Wal-Mart is either a registered trademark or trademark of Wal-Mart Stores, Inc. in the United States and/or other countries.

Xdrive is either a registered trademark or trademark of Xdrive LLC in the United States and/or other countries.

Yahoo! is either a registered trademark or trademark of Yahoo! Inc. in the United States and/or other countries.

Zone Labs and ZoneAlarm are either registered trademarks or trademarks of Check Point Software Technologies Ltd. in the United States and/or other countries.

Contents
At A Glance

o Buying
...ws Vista™
...me Office

an...
O...

Everything You Need to Know About:

- Buying a new computer
- Backups
- Anti-virus
- Anti-spyware...AND MUCH MORE!

[In a straightforward, easy to understand book.]

Just the Computer Essentials

by James A. White

A Plain-English, No-Nonsense Guide to Buying
and Maintaining a PC Running the Windows Vista™
Operating System for Your Home or Home Office

Published by IROL Press

IROL Press, LLC
http://www.irolpress.com

Just the Computer Essentials
First Edition

ISBN: 978-0-9792971-6-8

http://www.booksbyjim.com

Cover / Design and Layout by Lori A. Balogh

Trademarks Attribution:

Microsoft product screen shot(s) reprinted with permission from Microsoft Corporation.

Microsoft, Access, Aero, Excel, Hotmail, Internet Explorer, MS-DOS, Microsoft Live OneCare, Outlook, PowerPoint, SuperFetch, Windows, Windows Server, Windows NT, and Windows Vista are either registered trademarks or trademarks of Microsoft Corporation in the United States and/or other countries.

"Just the Computer Essentials" is an independent publication and is not affiliated with, nor has it been authorized, sponsored, or otherwise approved by Microsoft Corporation.

Adobe and Acrobat Reader are either registered trademarks or trademarks of Adobe Systems Incorporated in the United States and/or other countries.

Amazon is either a registered trademark or trademark of Amazon.com, Inc. in the United States and/or other countries.

AMD, Athlon, Sempron, and Turion are either registered trademarks or trademarks of Advanced Micro Devices, Inc. in the United States and/or other countries.

AOL is either a registered trademark or trademark of AOL LLC in the United States and/or other countries.

Apple, FireWire, Mac, Mac OS, and Macintosh are either registered trademarks or trademarks of Apple Inc. in the United States and/or other countries.

Belkin is either a registered trademark or trademark of Belkin International, Inc. in the United States and/or other countries.

Best Buy is either a registered trademark or trademark of Best Buy Concepts, Inc. in the United States and/or other countries.

Blu-Ray is either a registered trademark or trademark of Sony Corporation in the United States and/or other countries.

CA and eTrust are either registered trademarks or trademarks of CA International, Inc. in the United States and/or other countries.

Circuit City is either a registered trademark or trademark of Circuit City Stores West Coast, Inc. in the United States and/or other countries.

Cisco and Linksys are either registered trademarks or trademarks of Cisco Systems, Inc. in the United States and/or other countries.

Corel and WordPerfect are trademarks or registered trademarks of Corel Corporation and/or its subsidiaries in Canada, the United States and/or other countries.

Dell is either a registered trademark or trademark of Dell Inc. in the United States and/or other countries.

D-Link is either a registered trademark or trademark of D-Link Corporation in the United States and/or other countries.

EasyOffice is either a registered trademark or trademark of E-Press Corp in the United States and/or other countries.

eBay is either a registered trademark or trademark of eBay Inc. in the United States and/or other countries.

ePrompter is either a registered trademark or trademark of Tiburon Technology, Inc. in the United States and/or other countries.

Trademarks Attribution (continued):

Eudora is either a registered trademark or trademark of QUALCOMM Incorporated in the United States and/or other countries.

GoDaddy is either a registered trademark or trademark of GoDaddy Software in the United States and/or other countries.

Google, Gmail, Google Groups, and Froogle are either registered trademarks or trademarks of Google in the United States and/or other countries.

Grisoft and AVG are either registered trademarks or trademarks of Grisoft, s.r.o. LTD in the United States and/or other countries.

HD DVD is either a registered trademark or trademark of DVD Format/Logo Licensing Corporation in the United States and/or other countries.

Hormel and SPAM are either registered trademarks or trademarks of Hormel Foods, LLC in the United States and/or other countries.

HP is either a registered trademark or trademark of Hewlett-Packard Development Company, L.P. in the United States and/or other countries.

IBackup is either a registered trademark or trademark of Pro Softnet Corporation in the United States and/or other countries.

IBM, Lotus, and SmartSuite are either registered trademarks or trademarks of International Business Machines Corporation in the United States and/or other countries.

IEEE is either a registered trademark or trademark of Institute of Electrical and Electronics Engineers, Inc. in the United States and/or other countries.

IncrediMail is either a registered trademark or trademark of IncrediMail Ltd. in the United States and/or other countries.

Intel, Celeron, Core, and Pentium are either registered trademarks or trademarks of Intel Corporation in the United States and/or other countries.

Intuit, QuickBooks, and Quicken are either registered trademarks or trademarks of Intuit Inc. in the United States and/or other countries.

Kerio is either a registered trademark or trademark of Kerio Technologies Inc. in the United States and/or other countries.

Linux is either a registered trademark or trademark of Linus Torvalds in the United States and/or other countries.

McAfee and SpamKiller are either registered trademarks or trademarks of McAfee, Inc. in the United States and/or other countries.

Motorola is either a registered trademark or trademark of Motorola, Inc. in the United States and/or other countries.

Mozilla, FireFox, and Thunderbird are either registered trademarks or trademarks of Mozilla Foundation in the United States and/or other countries.

NETGEAR is either a registered trademark or trademark of NETGEAR, Inc. in the United States and/or other countries.

Contents
At A Glance (continued):

Expanded Table of Contents

Expanded Table
of Contents (continued):

Expanded Table
of Contents (continued):

Acknowledgements

When I first started writing this book, I never expected it to be as time consuming and as much hard work as it was. I wanted this book to be extremely thorough and as straightforward as possible. Because of this, I put a lot of time and effort into it. Unfortunately, it also took a lot of time away from those I care about. I got married to my girlfriend of six years while still in the midst of writing this. With that said, I want to dedicate this book to my wonderful wife, Lisa White. Lisa, I don't know how you put up with me while I was so engrossed in this book, but I love you so much for your patience as well as your support and encouragement. I would also like to extend my appreciation to my in-laws for the warm welcome into their family.

Of course, I wouldn't be where I am today without the support of my family - my mother Cookie, my father Frank, and my brother Joe. You've always been there whenever I needed help or support.

I'd also like to say thanks to Gary Ellis. You took a guy with no experience and gave me an opportunity to learn and grow as a systems engineer and later as the systems engineers' manager. I will always appreciate the chance you took in bringing me aboard.

Additionally, I want to express my appreciation to my cousin, Lori Balogh, for helping with the cover and the design and layout of this book. Lori, you definitely have an eye for this and I am grateful that you used that talent to help me with this book.

Finally, I want to thank those that helped review this book to ensure it was both accurate and understandable - Lisa White, Linda Kelly, and Dave Russell.

– Jim

Introduction

Some books are written that try to cover everything there is about computers. Other books are written that try to go into every detail about a very specific aspect of a single component in this vast world of technology. This book is different. This book was written for the typical end user - the person who uses a computer for everyday things. Most of us use a computer for things like email, instant messaging, digital pictures, and maybe Microsoft® Word or Excel® software. If you fall into this category, you probably have questions regarding buying a new computer, protecting your computer from viruses, or just some best practices like how to back up your computer data.

I'm going to help you understand what you need to know about computers without giving you too much information that you won't ever need to know.

I stumbled into the technology field accidentally. I was an art major at Kent State University in the early 90's. And although I thought I was pretty good at it, I was not very happy with the thought of doing this for a living. Then I ended up taking a class called *Intro to Computers* as an elective taught by a great professor - Geoffrey Steinberg. I became very intrigued and quickly changed my major to Computer Information Systems.

To help pay for school, I was working in retail where I soon started to "move up the ranks" to become an assistant store manager. As I was nearing the last year of school, I left retail because I knew I didn't want to do this for the rest of my life. I found a job at a company that gave me an opportunity. With no experience, I was lucky to gain a job as a Systems Engineer. I was brought in to help out in beating the infamous Y2K disaster about to strike! All right, it turned out not to be the disaster that was predicted, but it did help me get my foot in the door.

Over the next five years, I continued to learn everything I could about computers, networking, and programming and I gained several certifications. Then I moved up again, this time to manage the engineers. It's in this position that I began to realize that I am lucky to have a great talent... the understanding of the fundamentals of technology and the ability to convey these fundamentals to end users in a way they understand.

That is why we're here right now... I want to pass onto you enough knowledge that you feel comfortable with buying, working with, and maintaining your computer. I want you to know that any email, pictures, or other important data you have is safe without worrying about losing it all should your computer crash. I don't want to give you a bunch of information that you'll read and think, "You know, this is something I'm never going to need to know!"

As a person in the technology field, you often hear the infamous words from family and friends quite often... "Hey, you work with computers, right?" It starts out as a "quick question" and before long, you've just spent hours trying to get their computer cleaned of viruses and spyware, up to date with different software patches, and maybe set up to properly back up their data.

I used to wonder why there wasn't a decent book out there for the typical user. There are books for users that don't even know how to turn on a computer and then on the other side, there are books for technical people like me that want to know everything there is to know. But there never seemed to be a good book written for the average Joe - the person that uses their computer on a regular basis, but doesn't know what to look for when buying a new one... someone that needs to know how to protect their data from computer crashes and bad things like viruses.

I often thought (half-jokingly) that maybe I should just write a book to address all these things. Then over the years, I began to take that thought a little more seriously... why not take what I've learned and know, and convey these best practices without making it too complex to understand?!

You may notice that as you get further into the parts of the book discussing maintaining your computer, there is an abundance of screenshots - well over 200!! This is because I know that sometimes it's easier to understand things by seeing them than it is to just read about them.

This book focuses primarily on Windows Vista™, the newest operating system from Microsoft®. It replaces Windows XP, which began shipping in late 2001 - a dinosaur in the computer world. With some of the new security features, new functionality, and past trends, Windows Vista will likely quickly gain a strong share of the market. If you're running an older version of Windows®, it's probably almost time for you to get a new computer and this book will definitely help you out.

I've tried to arrange the content of this book in a way that will help make sense if you read it from cover to cover or if you just need help with something specific (like how to perform a backup in Windows Vista).

So, let's jump in and get started!!

I. The Basics of Buying a New Computer

chapter 1

Buying a New Computer

Every week, the Sunday newspaper is filled with an abundance of advertisements for different computers. Some are just a few hundred dollars, while others can cost thousands. Unless you know what to look for, you're generally stuck taking the word of a clerk in the store. Are you finding a good deal or are you going to get stuck with a computer that doesn't quite have the "oomph" for what you're trying to do? I want to help you understand what to look for. So let's go over some basics first.

Longevity

When buying a new computer, plan on a life expectancy of that computer to be around three to five years. This is usually the life cycle that a new computer will last you before it becomes more of a burden than a helpful tool. The reason this happens is that as time passes, your needs will change. Software developers look to find ways to make your life on the computer easier, which means creating updates and new versions of the programs you use. These updates and new versions require more of the computer's resources. So, over time, as you begin to use the software that helps accommodate your needs, you start to notice that the computer doesn't seem as fast as it once was. There are ways around this (buying more memory, a faster CPU, etc), but in general, with PCs continuing to drop in price, replacing the computer makes the most sense - similar to the dilemma of whether to fix a broken television or replace it. Usually it makes sense nowadays to replace a television versus having it fixed based on cost.

Hard drive versus memory

The difference between the hard drive and memory confuses many people. The hard drive is like a filing cabinet. This is where the operating system (OS) lives, such as Windows XP or Windows Vista™, as well as where all your data is saved. So, when you start your computer up and want to look at the pictures you copied from your digital camera or a letter that you typed up, you'll find them stored on the hard drive. It's just like documents being stored in a filing cabinet.

Hard drive storage continues to drop in price and you continue to get more for your money. Obviously, the bigger the hard drive, the more data you can save to it. Hard drives are generally referred to by the amount of data storage they can provide. For instance, a 250-gigabyte (GB) hard drive can hold up to 250 gigabytes of data.

What's a gigabyte? Well, to help understand, take a look at the following measurements comparison table...

MEASUREMENT	SIZE	EXAMPLES
Bit	1	The smallest unit of information in the computer world
Byte	8 Bits	If you opened up Notepad and typed in a single character and then saved the file, that would be about one byte
Kilobyte (KB)	1024 Bytes	Because Word and Excel documents store more than just what is typed (such as the formatting), even an empty file is around 10 to 20 kilobytes
Megabyte (MB)	1024 Kilobytes	Typically, the size of one or two digital pictures together equal one megabyte A CD can hold up to 700 MB of data
Gigabyte (GB)	1024 Mega-bytes	A standard DVD holds about 4.7 GB of data (or approximately the same amount of data as almost 7 CDs)
Terabyte	1024 Gigabytes	This is a lot of data! Most small/medium businesses don't consume a TB of data yet. However, this will change in the near future.

There are higher measurements (Petabyte, Exabyte, etc), but with the exception of businesses with extremely large storage needs, such as Microsoft, it is unlikely that you will hear too much about these data measurements for at least a couple more years.

As of right now, a hard drive of 200 GB or more is not uncommon for new desktop computers. For the average home user, a computer with a 200 GB hard drive should be sufficient for the computer you buy for a few years down the line. Keep in mind that Windows Vista itself will consume a good portion of this - plan on 10 to 15 GB.

Memory on a computer is different than the hard drive. Memory, also known as Random Access Memory or RAM, is much faster than the hard drive. This is because hard drives are similar to the way record players or CD players work. Hard drives contain a platter that spins, similar to a record or CD, and have an arm that reads the information from this platter.

RAM, on the other hand, consists of chips and the data is read or written electronically. Because RAM transfers data electronically versus using mechanics, RAM is much quicker than hard drives. However, RAM requires a constant electrical charge to hold its contents whereas a hard drive, which writes its contents magnetically, does not. So, if you shut off your computer, anything in RAM will be lost, but the information on the hard drive will remain.

When working on a computer and you save a file - let's use a Microsoft Word document in this example - it is saved to the hard drive where you can get to it whenever you need to. However, when you open the Word document to work on it, it would be excessively slow for each character you type to be written to the document on the hard drive. That's where RAM comes into play. When you open the Word document, a copy of the document actually is opened in RAM (the computer memory). This allows you to make real-time changes to the document very quickly. When you click "Save" to save the document, the Word software actually takes the document that is stored in RAM and writes it to the hard drive, overwriting the previous file that was stored there.

Remember that RAM is volatile and will lose its contents without power. So, if you were to shut off the computer before clicking "Save," any changes you made would be gone. Your new document, or changes you made to an existing document, are not saved to the hard drive until you click "Save."

Every program requires a chunk of memory to run. When the computer runs out of memory to use for open programs, it uses part of the hard drive to read and write what it would normally use RAM for. This slows a computer down tremendously. To be sure this doesn't happen, you want to be sure your computer has enough RAM in it.

CPU / Front Side Bus

The CPU, or Central Processing Unit, is considered the brains of the computer. It is also sometimes simply known as a computer's processor. This is where most calculations and logic of a computer take place. The CPU is measured by the speed in which it performs calculations. The faster the processor speed, the faster the CPU is able to perform calculations.

Currently, the two main competitors in the processor market are Intel® and AMD®, which continue to battle each other for market share. The most popular desktop CPUs from Intel were the Pentium® and Celeron® processors for many years, but these have recently been left behind for the new Intel Core™ processors. AMD continues to improve upon its Athlon® processor. Other common AMD processors are the Sempron® and the Turion®.

When looking for a new computer, you may notice that stores tend to try to sell you on the CPU speed of the computer. This used to be a very important factor when buying a computer - the faster the processor meant the faster the computer. Nowadays, however, the CPU has generally outdone some of the other components in regard to speed. That means that even though the processor can do the calculations quickly, it still needs to let the other components know what the results of the calculations are (such as RAM). If the other components can't keep up, then it doesn't matter too much how fast the processor is.

Because of this, an important number to look at when looking for a new computer is the Front Side Bus (FSB). The Front Side Bus is sometimes referred to as the Processor Bus, Memory Bus, or System Bus. The main function of the Front Side Bus is to link the CPU to the main memory. The faster the Front Side Bus, the faster it can move the information the processor has ready to go. This is why the processor speed and Front Side Bus speed go hand-in-hand. The faster these two are, the faster the computer generally will be.

As of right now, 2.8 GHz (gigahertz) on up is about the norm for a processor speed. For the Front Side Bus, anything less than a 500 MHz (megahertz) will end up holding up the processor speed and causing the computer to not seem as quick to react as it should. The Front Side Bus is usually listed as the FSB when looking at different computer models. So, when the computer salesperson tells you "This computer has a 3.2 GHz processor," your first response should be "Great - what's the speed of the Front Side Bus?"

Laptops

The name laptop is synonymous with notebook. Until recently, desktop computer sales have always surpassed laptop sales. This has changed now that laptops have continued to drop in price and can offer portability, convenience, and with many laptops, the power of a desktop computer. Should you consider buying a laptop instead of a desktop computer?

If you are purchasing a new computer specifically for playing intense computer or Internet games, you will most likely want to purchase a desktop computer. Desktops can be upgraded to provide the necessary video, audio, and processor capabilities.

In many other cases, you may want to consider a laptop over a desktop. Laptops now generally come standard with integrated wireless capabilities. When choosing an Internet Service Provider (ISP) for your Internet connection, such as DSL or cable, the ISP will most likely provide you with a wireless router free of charge. This will allow you to access the Internet throughout your house. If you want to be able to work (or play) away from home, a laptop is definitely the way to go.

If you are looking to get the best of both worlds, a docking station can be purchased for a laptop. A docking station is just what the name implies. A regular monitor, mouse, full size keyboard, and any other devices (such as a printer) are plugged into the docking station. The laptop can then be quickly connected to the docking station to take advantage of all the connected resources. This allows you the full-size resources of a desktop computer while at home and the convenience of a laptop by being able to easily disconnect it from the docking station and take it with you wherever you go.

Wireless

Wireless connectivity has continued to help the growth of home networks. Cost has dropped tremendously and allows home users (and businesses) to quickly enable multiple computers to share resources with each other, such as printers, files, and Internet connection without the need for wiring an entire house.

In order to provide interoperability between different companies, a standards committee called the Institute of Electrical and Electronics Engineers (IEEE®) help to define exactly how something will work. Input is usually contributed from major companies such as Cisco®, Microsoft, HP®, Motorola®, etc. Once a standard is defined, any company can incorporate the specifics of that standard into their products. This is extremely important for us as consumers because it provides the ability to not have to rely on one vendor for everything and instill confidence that they should work together. If I have devices, such as routers, from two different companies, they *should* be able to talk to each other seamlessly if both vendors followed the standards exactly. Now, I said "should" in italics a couple times because many times a vendor will take the standard and "tweak" things on it - maybe to gain something like speed for instance. This works great if you have one company supplying all the equipment, but if you have another company's devices in the picture, sometimes they don't always play nice together.

There are currently three major standards in the consumer wireless world right now - 802.11a, 802.11b, and 802.11g. Another standard, 802.11n, is expected to be approved in mid 2007. Each provides something a little different, as shown in the table on the following page.

	802.11a	802.11b	802.11g	802.11n
Speed	Up to 54 Mbps*	Up to 11 Mbps*	Up to 54 Mbps*	Up to 540 Mbps*
Frequency	5 GHz band - Less crowded frequency	2.4 GHz band - More crowded frequency - Many cell phones operate on this frequency and devices can interfere with one another	2.4 GHz band - More crowded frequency - Many cell phones operate on this frequency and devices can interfere with one another	2.4 GHz band - More crowded frequency; Can also operate on 5 GHz band - Less crowded frequency
Range	Generally 25-75 feet indoors, depending on room layout and types of walls	Generally 100-150 feet indoors, depending on room layout and types of walls	Generally 100-150 feet indoors, depending on room layout and types of walls	Roughly 160 feet indoors, depending on room layout and types of walls
Compatibility	Incompatible with 802.11b and 802.11g	Incompatible with 802.11a, but 802.11g devices can downgrade themselves to work with 802.11b devices	Compatible with 802.11b by downgrading themselves, but not with 802.11a	Compatible with 802.11b and 802.11g by downgrading themselves, but not with 802.11a

Mbps is short for Megabits per second. This is the speed at which data can be transferred.

In stores now, you will likely see 802.11g as the standard the stores and manufacturers push. This makes sense because it provides the faster speed and the larger range. So, when looking for a new laptop, try to make sure that 802.11g wireless capabilities are built into it.

In most cases, here's how wireless connectivity generally comes into play. Let's say you have a desktop computer, two laptop computers, and a printer. This is probably more computers than most people have at home, but it's good for our example. In addition, it helps you understand things if you are a small business owner. Let's also say you have purchased DSL as your connection to the Internet.

Here's what I would generally consider the best method to set things up. You can purchase a small wireless router that supports 802.11g with maybe a 4-port switch built into it. This will likely run you in the neighborhood of $50 from a company such as Linksys®, D-Link®, or NETGEAR® that you can purchase from your local Best Buy®, Wal-Mart®, or reputable online vendor. This may even be something that the ISP gives you with your DSL agreement.

Then you connect the DSL router to the new wireless router. Now devices that connect to the wireless router can get out to the Internet. In our example, the two laptops with the 802.11g wireless capabilities can get out to the Internet from usually about 100 to 150 feet away from the wireless router. By plugging in the desktop computer to the built-in 4-port switch on the wireless router, the desktop computer can now also get out to the Internet. Take a look at the diagram to see what I'm talking about.

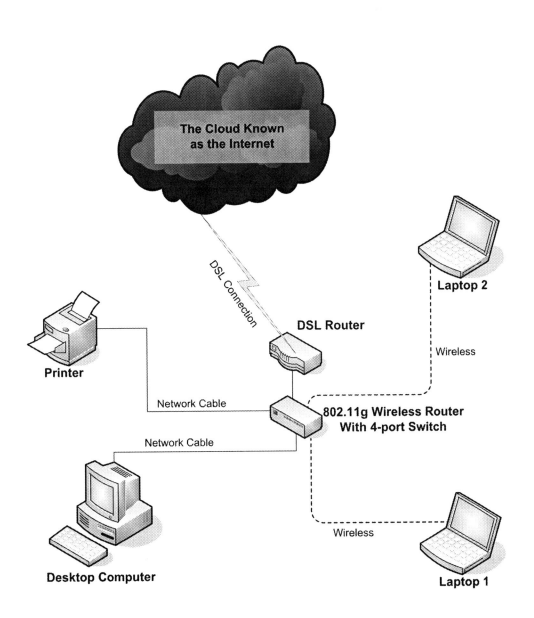

And, because everything comes together to the central wireless router, the devices connected are now capable of communicating with each other. That means files can be transferred from a laptop to the desktop computer, or laptop to laptop, or whatever. You can prevent a device from being accessed by security means, but the point is the communication ability is now available should you want to use it.

If the printer has a network port on it, it can also be connected to the 4-port switch of the wireless router. Now users from either laptop or the desktop computer can all print to the same printer. If the printer does not have a network port, the printer can stay connected to the desktop computer and be shared through the computer. Users can now still print to the printer (in this case, though, since you are going through the desktop computer, it must be turned on).

There - you've now built a home network! That wasn't so bad, was it?

Also, please keep in mind that new technologies are being developed all the time. In fact, the wireless standard, 802.11n, will be out shortly after this book is published and will offer speeds of over 500Mbps! There are many vendors currently releasing "Pre-N" equipment right now, which is designed around what "might" become the standard, but this equipment is not guaranteed to work with the new standard once it is approved and all changes have been made. The standard is expected to be approved soon and equipment based off the new standard should begin to quickly follow.

Operating System

In order to do anything with a computer, you need an operating system, sometimes referred to as an OS. The operating system is there, in essence, to be the foundation for the computer. It allows other programs to run, takes care of accepting keyboard and mouse input, keeps track of all the files on the computer's hard drive, and acts as a traffic cop to help ensure that programs do not conflict with each other. It's a big job, but somebody's got to do it!

As you may know, Microsoft rules the PC market with its Windows® operating systems, such as Windows XP and Windows Vista. There are other alternatives out there, such as the Linux® operating system, which gets a lot of press, but is not currently the most user-friendly for the average user. There are also not as many software applications that run on it yet. The Linux OS is what is considered open-source. This means that anyone can view the programming code behind it and is welcome to recommend changes. There is a very strong following and many different flavors of the Linux OS have emerged. Probably sometime relatively soon, it may begin to take off even more quickly and become a stronger alternative to the Windows operating system. However, until that time comes, I would recommend sticking with the latest and greatest from Microsoft. Microsoft has had its share of bad press due to problems with security, but they have worked to rebuild that image by focusing on making security a top priority.

Apple® also has its hand in the operating system business with its Mac® line of computers. Macintosh® computers are a little different because you cannot just install the Mac OS® (operating system) on a PC you pick up from the store. The Mac computer is both an operating system and hardware. When you buy a Mac computer, you're buying both. The primary strong point of the Mac OS used to be graphics and audio. In the past, when you were a graphics designer, you would never think about using something other than a Mac computer. The times have changed however, and the Windows OS is considered by many to be able to do almost everything the Mac OS can do with graphic design. Our focus for this book, however, is with the IBM-compatible PCs, meaning they are based off the IBM® architecture, which is the hardware the Windows OS runs on. As a side note, Mac computers have now started to move to the Intel chipset making it possible to run the Mac OS or the Windows OS on the same hardware. This, however, is outside the scope of what we're trying to accomplish in this book.

Microsoft recently released its newest flagship operating system called Windows Vista. After working with both the pre-releases of the Windows Vista operating system for quite some time, as well as the actual release, I would strongly recommend that when purchasing a new computer, you ensure that it comes with the Windows Vista OS and not a previous version of Windows.

There are a number of reasons that I recommend this:

Security - Microsoft has now gotten to the point where they know how to build a stable operating system. It has, however, realized that its weakest point has been security. In the Windows XP operating system (the version of Windows before Windows Vista), Microsoft developed a Service Pack (SP2) that helped make Windows XP a more secure operating system. The problem is that it is much more difficult to add security to a product after the fact rather than to design a product with security in mind. Microsoft has also realized this and has designed the Windows Vista OS from the ground up with security as its foremost thought.

Support - Microsoft puts all its products on a lifecycle including the point where it will no longer support it. This is because as new technologies come out, older products may no longer be compatible. In addition, they become harder for Microsoft to support. And of course, it helps Microsoft to push users to buy their new products, which will drive their business. Because Windows Vista is the latest operating system, its lifecycle is just beginning and will continue to be supported by Microsoft. If vulnerabilities or problems are discovered, new patches will continue to be released to help overcome them.

Features - The Windows Vista OS is current. It's been designed to accommodate other new technologies: better built-in wireless integration and security (generally for laptops), Volume Shadow Copies (a feature that provides automatic backups of files on a regular basis), integrated indexing and desktop search (find a file instantly by just knowing a key word or two in the document), etc. There are an abundance of new features that are built in to help Microsoft sell its new operating system. Normally I don't suggest buying a new operating system just because of the bells and whistles. Nevertheless, if you're going to get a new computer, why not get some of the latest features as well?

Unlike its predecessor, which had two versions - a Home Edition and a Professional Edition, Microsoft released six editions of this product. These editions will be put under the categories of consumer, business, and emerging markets. Here is the lowdown on the different Windows Vista OS editions offered:

Emerging Market Editions

Windows Vista Starter Edition - This is a severely crippled version of the Windows Vista OS, meaning much of the functionality is not available. It is designed for third world countries to start to become familiar with the Windows operating system. It limits almost everything and even if it were available in the U.S., I would not recommend this for any home or business user.

Business Editions

Windows Vista Business Edition - This edition is comparable to the Windows XP Professional OS. It supports joining a Windows domain, file encryption (EFS), and Remote Desktop, among other things. If you are in a business environment that has a Windows domain, you need this version and should not try to cut costs by getting a home version. It will come back and bite you in the long run.

Windows Vista Enterprise Edition - Enterprise Edition adds unique features to the Windows Vista Business Edition such as Virtual PC, full volume encryption, and the Multi-language User Interface (MUI). It is designed with large business enterprise users in mind and is only available to Software Assurance customers.

Consumer Editions

Windows Vista Home Basic Edition - This version is designed to be marketed toward general consumers. It is what would be considered the Windows XP Home Edition operating system equivalent. It is extremely stripped down and I generally would not recommend this version to most users.

Windows Vista Home Premium Edition - The Home Premium Edition contains everything Home Basic includes as well as focusing on some other features such as stronger media capabilities (DVD video authoring, DVD ripping support, etc), Tablet PC support, and some enhanced networking capabilities, among other things. This version is aimed more toward homes with more than one computer (to allow for simpler networking), as well as for homes with children (unified parental controls), and laptop users (additional wireless capabilities and other mobility features).

And last but not least...

Windows Vista Ultimate Edition - This is the "everything" version of the Windows Vista OS. Ultimate Edition includes everything the Home and Business Editions have as well as the Game Performance Tweaker, a utility to create podcasts, some included online services, etc. This version is marketed for digital media enthusiasts, gamers, and "techies" in general.

As a side note, there are also the "N" Editions, which are an additional offering for the European market to meet the requirement of an antitrust suit. These are the same as the Home Basic and Business Editions, but do not include Windows Media Player.

So... with all of the different versions offered, how do you know which edition is right for you? Well, as I mentioned above, if you are in a business environment, you probably don't want to skimp by getting a Home version. I've had more than one client that has gone the route (without consulting someone in the business) of buying the Windows XP Home Edition operating system for their business computer. When I got to the customer site to provide support for problems, it turned out to be problems that could easily have been avoided by purchasing the Windows XP Professional OS. Instead, the client had the choice of buying the upgrade to the Professional version or having me charge for my support time to provide a workaround. Both solutions cost the customer more money than they would have spent if they had simply purchased the correct version to start with.

To give you a better idea of which version is right for you, here is a comparison chart of some of the differences between each of the editions:

	Home Basic	Home Premium	Business	Enterprise	Ultimate
Windows BitLocker drive encryption				Yes	Yes
Windows Ultimate Extras					Yes
Ability To Join Domain			Yes	Yes	Yes
Encrypting File System (EFS)			Yes	Yes	Yes
IIS Web Services			Yes	Yes	Yes
Remote Desktop (to be able to remotely connect to your computer)			Yes	Yes	Yes
Windows Complete PC Backup and Restore			Yes	Yes	Yes
Windows Fax and Scan			Yes	Yes	Yes
DVD Video Authoring		Yes			Yes
Windows Media Center		Yes			Yes
Windows Movie Maker (including support for the HD format)		Yes			Yes
Windows Aero™ Graphics Interface		Yes	Yes	Yes	Yes
Scheduled backups		Yes	Yes	Yes	Yes
Tablet PC Support		Yes	Yes	Yes	Yes

	Home Basic	Home Premium	Business	Enterprise	Ultimate
Windows Flip 3D / Taskbar thumbnails		Yes	Yes	Yes	Yes
Maximum number of processors supported	1	2	2	2	2
Maximum amount of RAM supported on 32-bit systems	4 GB	4 Gb	4 GB	4 GB	4 GB
Maximum amount of RAM supported on 64-bit systems	8 GB	16 GB	128 GB+	128 GB+	128 GB+
Windows Mobility Center	Limited	Limited	Yes	Yes	Yes
Parental Controls	Yes	Yes			

Software

When you buy a new computer, you will notice that it comes with a lot of software already installed - some good and plenty of junk that you will probably never use. Software is usually referred to as an application or program that runs on the computer. Everything from the Microsoft Word and Excel programs to large financial packages like the Quicken®, Microsoft Money, and QuickBooks® programs down to a simple tool like the Microsoft calculator are all software. The price of applications can range anywhere from free to thousands of dollars and these can add up quickly. Before going to the store and grabbing every piece of software off the shelf to go with your new computer, I would like to suggest that you wait until you determine your needs. You may already have a similar application that comes preinstalled on your computer that does everything you need.

Peripherals

We could talk about all the extras that computers have for days, so instead I'll go over the important things that might be considered important when getting a new computer.

The first is the CD/DVD drive. When you get a new computer, you will most likely have several options for what you want this device to do, so let's go over some of the choices...

CD-ROM - The ROM part stands for (Read-Only Memory), the key being "read-only." A CD-ROM will let you install software from CDs, play music CDs (assuming you have sound in your computer), etc. But that's about it. You cannot burn CDs with this. It's almost impossible to find a new computer nowadays that can't burn CDs.

CD-RW - Here the RW stands for (Read-Write). With a CD-RW drive, you can buy either CD-R disks or CD-RW disks. The former will let you burn a CD one time and if you don't like it, you can pitch it. The latter will allow you to erase what was on the CD-RW and write over it. CD-RW disks did not become as popular as anticipated because the price of blank CD-R disks dropped to practically pennies. A CD-RW drive also has the read function, so you can also play music and install software just like a CD-ROM will let you do.

DVD-ROM - Similar to the CD-ROM, the DVD-ROM will allow you to play DVDs (and CDs).

DVD+/-RW - When DVD burning started to become popular, different formats began appearing (DVD+R, DVD+RW, DVD-RAM, DVD-R, DVD-RW). This was similar to the VHS/Beta war back when VCR's first appeared. However, in this case, a single standard did not become the winner. So different vendors now back different standards. With a DVD+/-RW drive, you should be able to play or record to any of the different DVD formats and play CD-ROMs as well.

Combo Drives - Combo drives combine two technologies to be able to do more than one function. For example, a CD-RW / DVD-ROM combo drive will allow you to burn and play CDs as well as play DVDs.

In many cases, you may want to look at having more than one drive on a new computer. If you want to be able to copy a CD for instance, you should consider getting (for example) a CD-ROM drive and a CD-RW drive. By utilizing the two, you can copy directly from one to the other. If you had only a CD-RW, you could still copy a CD, but you would need to first copy the CD to a temporary location on the hard drive and then burn it to a CD.

DVD burning has not taken off as widely as CD burning did. It is still an extremely nice feature to have however, but one that may not be that important to you. A blank DVD can hold 4.7 GB of data whereas a CD can only hold 700 MB (almost seven times less data). Looking back, I've only ever burned a handful of DVDs in my entire technical career. However, I've burned hundreds of data CDs. Technology conveniences such as USB flash drives have likely helped to stifle the growth.

The speed of each of the components used to be a huge factor when purchasing any of the burning products. For example, a 12x CD burner versus a 24x CD burner was a huge difference. Nowadays, when you buy a new computer, you can feel relatively confident that you're getting a fast burner. So, I wouldn't worry too much about the speeds, but for your own knowledge, here is what the numbers mean. When you see numbers, such as 12x or 24x talking about a CD/DVD unit, this refers to the drive's data transfer rate called the drive rating. A data transfer rate of 1x is equal to 150 KBps (kilobytes per second), 2x is equal to 300 KBps, 3x is equal to 600 KBps, etc. CD-ROM or DVD-ROM drives will have a single drive rating which tells you how fast they can read the data. In a burner unit, there will usually be three numbers such as 48x, 24x, 48x. This would tell you the unit has a write speed of 48x, a rewrite speed of 24x, and a read speed of 48x.

Many PCs will offer deals that come with a basic, free printer. This may be sufficient for some users, while others may require something more robust. For nearly all home or small business users, there are a few types of printers that may be applicable.

The basic inkjet printer will suit most home users. Modern inkjet printers have become very streamlined. They spray a jet of ink onto the page to form the letters/graphics and call it a day. The newer inkjet printers are sometimes labeled as photo printers. These printers have been designed for printing digital photographs and work very well. With a high-quality printout, it can even be hard to tell the difference between that or an actual photograph. These printers can print usually somewhere in the range of 8 to 30 ppm (pages per minute) in black and white or 8 to 22 ppm in color. These types of printers should be sufficient for the majority of home users.

You may find that the ink cartridge(s) that comes with the computer will not last long. This is because they are generally only partially filled. Often times the manufacturer sells the printer for a very low profit intending on making up the profit on the printer cartridges they sell. Consider the cost of new ink cartridges when choosing a printer.

The next type of printer is a laser printer. The concept of how these work is somewhat involved, but for our purposes here, they basically burn the image onto the paper using toner. These work much faster than an inkjet printer does. Laser printers usually print somewhere in the area of 15 to 50 ppm (pages per minute) for a black and white laser printer. There are color laser printers available that print around 4 to 27 ppm in color. Again, look at the cost of replacing the toner cartridge when considering your printer.

Another type of printer is the "all-in-one" or multifunction printer. These are designed to meet the needs of users to get the convenience of multiple functions in one device. They usually provide the ability to print (as a laser printer), fax, copy, and scan all from the one device. These usually print around 15 ppm to 20 ppm for a home-use black and white printer or around 10 to 20 ppm with a home-use color multifunction printer. Faster, more powerful multifunction printers are also available, designed specifically to target small business owners.

Monitors have changed over the past year or so. Until recently, CRT (cathode-ray-tube) monitors were your only choice when buying. These are the monitors that are deeper and larger in depth, similar to televisions that have been predominant until recently. Like televisions though, technology is changing. Flat panel computer monitors are significantly thinner in size, similar to plasma and LCD televisions that have become popular lately and are now quickly becoming the norm.

Flat panel monitors, known as LCD (liquid crystal display) monitors are attractive for a few reasons. The most obvious is the space you save on your desk to fill with other good junk! They also provide a brighter picture than a CRT monitor and provide for crisper text and sharper images. In addition, they can actually help save in energy costs because they use only about a third of the wattage a CRT monitor uses.

So why not get a flat panel monitor? Well, the biggest downside is cost - a flat panel monitor will cost you more than a CRT monitor. The good news is that due to demand, that cost gap is quickly diminishing. Another thing to consider is that LCDs don't refresh as quickly as CRT monitors do. This isn't something you'll notice for the majority of tasks (Office applications, Internet surfing, Email, etc), but for something like the heavy gamer, the latency may be noticed.

Personally, I like the flat panel LCD monitors better than the larger CRT monitors. However, I would recommend that before purchasing a flat panel monitor for the first time, you head up to a Best Buy or Circuit City® and look at the monitor to determine if it is something you feel would be right for you. Check it at a resolution (the size of things on the screen) that you are comfortable with, as well as at the same angle you will be looking at it once purchased (due to how LCDs can be difficult to view at different angles).

The last peripheral I wanted to mention is the floppy drive. The floppy drive is the device on the computer in which the 3.5" square floppy disks that was used to save out data to take with you or back up from the computer. This used to be a must-have on any computer. However, almost all new computers now come with a CD burner (or in many cases, a DVD burner). One CD holds the equivalent of well over 450 floppy disks! And CDs are extremely cheap (you can find a spindle of 50 for less than $10 after rebates!). This has made floppy drives less important.

Then, USB flash drives started to become popular. These are the small devices that are usually not much larger than the size of a key (in fact many are designed as keychains). These are electronic and considered more reliable than floppy disks or CDs. It is currently common to see these in sizes of 1 gigabyte (GB) up to 8 GB (and still getting larger). To give you an idea, 2 GB flash drives are now very common. One of these 2 GB drives has the capacity equivalent of almost 3 CDs or over 1,400 floppy disks - all on a little keychain!

Due to the convenience, reliability, and capacity of USB flash drives, the floppy drive is now becoming a legacy device. Computer vendors have been following one another in making public statements that they will no longer have the floppy drive as a standard device on their PCs. Many vendors will let you purchase a floppy drive as an accessory, but once you've taken any data you may have on floppy disks and moved it elsewhere, you'll probably never need a floppy drive on a new computer. If you need to move data from place to place, though, I would however look at getting a USB flash drive. As of this writing, a 2 GB flash drive will run you less than $100. In addition, by press time, the cost will have dropped significantly and the capacity increased.

<u>Warranties</u>

When buying a new computer, you will want to be sure to observe the warranty. Not all warranties are created equal. You may find some warranties provide you 90 days, while some will provide you 1 year or 3 years. Some offer parts, some labor. Some offer extended warranties. Some provide onsite and some don't... you get the picture! Take a step back and think about what makes the most sense for you. In most cases, a good bet is to go with a 2-year onsite warranty if available for a decent price. Anything less can end up costing you a good chunk of money if you have a problem within a year or so of getting your computer. Anything longer than a 3-year warranty is probably not going to be worth it. Remember how fast technology changes. As I mentioned before, a computer's lifespan is about 3 to 5 years. It doesn't make sense to buy insurance for something you're probably not going to have for much longer after that.

The onsite part is also important for most people. If you're a technical guru on the hardware insides of a computer, then this will probably not apply to you. But for most people, if a support technician determines over the phone that you have a bad processor and sends you a new processor with a heat sink, you're not going to know what to do with it! And that's where the onsite part makes a lot more sense. The onsite warranty means that the computer manufacturer will send someone to take care of things for you when (and it's usually a "when" and not an "if") you start having computer hardware problems.

Be careful, too. There are many warranties that will offer you a 3-year warranty, first year onsite. That's OK - but remember, after that first year, you might be the one trying to figure out what goes where. So just do what makes sense for you.

Summary - Putting it all together

Now that we've gone through many of the basics, let's try to recap on a lot of this, so you can go out and get that new computer!

Here's a sample table that will help guide you on the major things to look for. This chapter should have already helped you determine which things you need to beef up and which things you might be able to somewhat cut back on:

Examples	Basic Desktop PC	Workhorse Desktop PC	Standard Notebook	Desktop Replacement Notebook
What this is...	Used for basics: Internet, Email, Digital Photos, etc.	Used for multi-tasking - Running many applications at once; Used by businesses or power users	Used for basics: Internet, Email, Digital Photos, etc.	Used for multi-tasking - Running many applications at once; Used by businesses or power users
Processor (CPU)	Intel Core 2 Duo; or AMD Athlon 64 X2 Dual-Core	Intel Core 2 Duo; or AMD Athlon 64 X2 Dual-Core	Intel Core 2 Duo; or AMD Sempron	Intel Core 2 Duo; or AMD Turion 64 X2 Dual-Core
Operating System	Microsoft Windows Vista Home Basic	Microsoft Windows Vista Home Premium	Microsoft Windows Vista Business	Microsoft Windows Vista Ultimate
Memory (RAM)	1 GB to 2 GB	2 GB to 4 GB	1 GB to 2 GB	2 GB to 4 GB
Hard Drive	160 GB (7200 rpm) SATA hard drive	250 GB (7200 rpm) SATA hard drive	80 GB (5400 rpm) SATA hard drive	120 GB (5400 rpm) SATA hard drive
Networking	10/100 Base-T Ethernet	10/100/1000 Base-T Ethernet	10/100 Base-T Ethernet	10/100/1000 Base-T Ethernet
Built-in Wireless			802.11b/g	802.11a/b/g
Optical Drive	Double-layer DVD+/-RW/CD-RW	Double-layer DVD+/-RW/CD-RW	Double-layer DVD+/-RW/CD-RW	Double-layer DVD+/-RW/CD-RW
Warranty	1-Year Limited Warranty, At-Home Service, and Tech Support plus Nights and Weekends	3-Year Limited Warranty, At-Home Service, and Tech Support plus Nights and Weekends	1-Year Limited Warranty, At-Home Service, and Tech Support plus Nights and Weekends	3-Year Limited Warranty, At-Home Service, and Tech Support plus Nights and Weekends

II. The Basics in Computer Hardware

chapter 2

Hard Drives

<u>What are they?</u>

As discussed earlier, the hard drive is where all the data on your computer gets saved. It is also where the operating system, such as Windows, resides. The hard drive is non-volatile, which means that the data is not lost when the computer is turned off.

Without getting into too much detail, a hard drive, for the most part, consists of a platter or a stack of more than one platter that stores data on both sides. The platter spins and a drive arm can then go from the outside of the platter to the inner circle of the platter similar to the way a record player works. As the drive arm moves, data can be read or written to the sides of the platter using electromagnetism. There is a drive arm and head for each side of the platter. The following diagram may help better visualize how this works.

Basic Mechanics of a Hard Drive

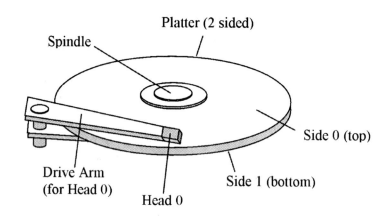

Spindle
Platter (2 sided)
Side 0 (top)
Drive Arm (for Head 0)
Side 1 (bottom)
Head 0

Hard Drive Tracks & Sectors

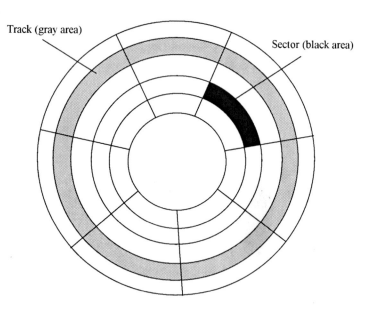

Track (gray area)
Sector (black area)

The hard drive platter is then divided into logical units called tracks that circle the surface of the platter and then further divided into sectors. Take a look at the following diagram for an idea of the concept of looking straight down at a hard drive platter.

You might be asking, "Who cares about tracks and sectors? What good does that do me?" Well, I could get more technical, but I just want to make sure you have a basic understanding of the concept of how hard drives work. The importance of understanding this lies in two important points:

1. Hard drives are mechanical devices. Although they are less prone to failure than they were in the past, failures DO occur. It's just like buying a new vacuum cleaner. Chances are you won't have any problems when you first get it. But if you have a problem with a new vacuum cleaner, you return it and get a new one. Same with a hard drive - except the manufacturer probably can't give you back all your data (documents, photos, etc.).

2. Data is stored in sectors. If a sector is 512 bytes long and a file that is 750 bytes needs to be saved to the hard drive, two 512 bytes are needed, or 1,024. 1,024 minus the 750 bytes needed for the data leaves 274 byes of wasted space. In addition, let's say you go back to that same file and add more information to it and it now becomes 3,500 bytes. It must now be saved to the hard drive and contiguous sectors (sectors next to each other) may not be available. In that case, sectors from elsewhere on the drive will be needed and used. Now you have a file in which parts are scattered on the hard drive. This is called fragmentation and slows performance because the head must go to different parts of the drive to access the data. A severely fragmented drive can seriously hinder performance. Because of that, defragmenting the hard drive can help make files contiguous on the hard drive and help performance. Windows Vista is the first operating system from Microsoft that, by default, does this automatically (on a weekly basis).

Formatting

In order for a hard drive to be used, it must first be formatted. Formatting is essentially just a means of preparation. When a hard drive is formatted, all data is erased from the drive. Then (depending on the formatting options), all sectors on the drive are examined and tested to make sure they are good. If a sector is found to be bad, it is marked appropriately so the operating system knows not to write data to that part of the hard drive. Finally, formatting creates address tables that will be used later to locate information as needed.

When you hear someone say they are going to reformat their computer and reinstall Windows, they're doing just that. They are backing up the data they want to save (hopefully!), then formatting the computer to erase everything on it - Windows and all data. Then they reinstall Windows from scratch and restore the data that they backed up.

Why would someone want to reformat his or her hard drive? Well, over time, you may notice that the Windows operating system starts to get sluggish or starts to have problems. Spyware on the computer may be slowing things down, a problem virus may have gotten out of control and delete critical files, software that was installed may possibly be conflicting with other software, there may be bad fragmentation on the drive, etc. Formatting a computer and reinstalling the operating system wipes everything clean and gives you a fresh start. It also allows for another check for bad sectors that may have crept up on the drive. It's a time consuming thing to do because the Windows OS needs to be reinstalled, along with every piece of software that you use. Then all the customizations that you like need to be redone. In the long run though, this can make a huge difference to have done every year or two.

They don't last forever

Hard drives should probably be considered by you, the end user, to be the most important part of a computer. Why? Because that's where you keep everything you save on the computer - digital pictures, maybe Word documents and Excel spreadsheets, email, and so on. That's why it's important to always remember that hard drives don't last forever. As with all mechanical devices, they WILL go bad eventually. Newer drives are designed better and generally last longer, but they will eventually go bad. Never consider data saved on your hard drive to be safe or you will most likely find yourself in a world of trouble the day your computer's hard drive says its final farewell.

If a sector is found to be bad, this means a physical problem exists in that location. Maybe there is a scratch or some other problem. All hard drives will have some bad sectors. This is not necessarily a concern unless there are a lot of bad sectors. If that is the case, then that may very well be a sign that the drive is going bad and should be replaced.

New computers

Hard drives come in different speeds. A faster speed means the hard drive spins faster. This also generally means that because it is spinning faster, data can be read or written to it more quickly. To be honest, for most users, the speed of the hard drive that is offered as the standard on a new computer should be fast enough.

Hard drives also come in different sizes. The larger the capacity of the hard drive, the more data it can store. For the majority of casual users, an 80 or 120 GB hard drive should suffice for the life of the computer. If, however, you plan to download tons of music (I'm talking thousands of songs) and tons of high-resolution digital pictures or doing video editing, you should definitely be looking at a 120 GB hard drive or larger.

Keep in mind that the Windows operating system alone will take a good portion of the hard drive. This could be anywhere from 5 GB to 15 GB. Your programs will also take up hard drive space - some more than others do.

In summary, make sure you remember the importance of your computer's hard drive. Make sure the hard drive you get has enough capacity for your data needs (with room to grow). Plan for the drive to go bad by being sure to back up your data on a regular basis (we'll discuss this later in the book). Moreover, let the Windows Vista operating system automatically handle the tidy work for you by defragmenting the drive and maintaining or improving performance.

chapter 3

RAM (Computer Memory)

What is it?

When you are working on a document in the Microsoft Word software, composing an email in the Microsoft Outlook® or Outlook Express programs, or playing Solitaire, you are working in RAM. RAM, short for Random Access Memory, is generally referred to as memory. RAM is kind of like a holding place for active programs.

Once you click on Save in a Word document for example, the operating system takes the information that is in RAM and writes it to a file on the hard drive. If you continue to work on the document, you are still working in RAM. Clicking Save again will dump the information from RAM again to the hard drive, this time overwriting the document that was there previously. If you pulled the power cable on your computer before clicking on Save a second time, when you start up the computer and reopen the document, you would see that everything is there from the first time you clicked Save, but you would have lost all new changes. This is because the RAM was not instructed to save out the new changes to the hard drive.

NOTE: Microsoft has learned that people sometimes forget to save documents as they go, so newer versions of the Microsoft Word software will now automatically save a backup copy of the document periodically. If the power went out, the next time you opened the Word software, it would likely help you bring back the most current version of the file it saved. This feature from Microsoft is called AutoRecover and is NOT a replacement for saving a document.

So why doesn't the operating system just write everything to the hard drive as we go and forget this whole RAM thing? Well, remember that RAM is much faster than a hard drive because RAM is not mechanical like a hard drive. RAM is electronic. If we didn't have computer memory (RAM) in place, your computer would be so slow it would be almost unusable.

So, can I run out of RAM? In a manner of speaking, yes. Every program that you open uses RAM to accomplish whatever the programmer wanted it to do. In the case of the Microsoft Word software, the document you see on the screen is using a chunk of RAM. The operating system (such as Windows) uses quite a bit of RAM just for its regular tasks. RAM is finite too, meaning that you only have so much. If you have 256 MB of RAM - maybe the operating system is using 100 MB, the Word application might be using 50 MB, and other programs running in the background might be using, let's say 156 MB. So that's all of the 256 MB of RAM in use - what would happen if I now decided to open up the Internet Explorer® web browser?

Remember when I mentioned that if we didn't have RAM, your computer would be extremely slow? Well, that's what would happen in a case like this. The operating system, by default, puts aside a section of the hard drive aside for use by what's called the page file or swap file. The page file is there to act as memory if need be. So in our example, when the Internet Explorer browser would open, it would need memory in order to present the browser to you on the screen. The operating system would then let it use the page file as if it was RAM. So now every time you're trying to do anything in the Internet Explorer browser, a page request would be done. Information that would normally be accessed in the extremely fast RAM is now being written, read from, and deleted from the hard drive. Suddenly everything slows to a crawl.

Fortunately, when you close programs, they (if they're programmed correctly) will release the RAM they were using, so other programs can use it. Unfortunately, the programs you see open in the taskbar along the bottom are not even close to all the programs running on your computer. There are likely to be another thirty, forty, or even more processes running in the background that you don't even know about or see. Keep in mind that spyware and viruses all run in RAM as well.

Maybe at one time you downloaded and installed a player for movie clips. Unbeknownst to you, the movie player's programmers may have decided that it would make more sense to have some of the player's components stay resident in memory (even when the main program isn't open). This way when you opened up the player, it would launch much quicker. Arguably, that may make sense. However, when you have a good dozen or more applications doing this, you lose a great deal of RAM before the actual programs are even open.

How much do I need?

It should now make more sense as to why having enough RAM in a computer is vital to its operation. In most environments, a computer running the Windows XP operating system will need somewhere between 512 MB and 1 GB to operate smoothly. Under the new operating system, Windows Vista, the Microsoft requirements are a minimum of 512 MB to be Windows Vista Capable or 1 GB of RAM to be Windows Vista Premium Capable (to take advantage of new features such as the Windows Aero user interface). In my field, you learn quickly that these requirements are to let you know that this is the requirement only if you planned to leave your computer sit and not do a thing on it... no software, no emailing, nothing.

A good rule of thumb has always been to ensure you at least double the requirements of Microsoft. In this case, that would mean you would want at least 1 to 2 GB of RAM in order to be able to run most programs without problems. However If you're a power user and like to have a dozen things going on the computer at once or plan to do some intense video editing, you will probably be better off with more RAM.

Keep in mind that you can always add more RAM to a computer later. If you haven't done it before, you would be very surprised at just how easy it is to add memory to a computer. You basically just pull the computer cover off and put the RAM stick into one of the open slots designed for it. When you start the computer, it will likely tell you it sees more memory in the computer and will ask you if that's OK. That's all there is to it.

The thing to keep in mind when purchasing a new computer is the number of slots the computer has built into it. For example, when looking at the computer's description, you may see that it has two memory slots in it and allows a maximum of 2 GB. Maybe it comes with 512 MB of RAM already in it. Therefore, you know that that 512 MB is already occupying at least one of those two memory slots. I say at least one because it's possible that instead of having one 512 MB RAM stick there are two 256 MB RAM sticks. In that case, both slots would be filled.

So in this example, if I want to have 2 GB of RAM in my computer, I then need to think about this. Let's say I find out that the 512 MB of RAM the computer came with is occupying one slot. That means I still need 1.5 GB (or 1,536 MB) more RAM (2 GB is the same as 2048 MB - review the table in "Chapter 1 - Buying a New Computer" for more information). Well, RAM doesn't come in 1.5 GB sticks. I could get a 1 GB stick, but with the other stick that's in there, that would only give me 1.5 GB, not the 2 GB I want. Chances are, what I would need to do is get two 1 GB sticks and remove the 512 MB stick that's already in there. The two 1 GB sticks of RAM would then give me the 2 GB that I wanted.

As a side note, you might think why don't you get a 2 GB stick of RAM to use with the 512 MB stick that's already in there? That would give you 2.5 GB. Well, it would, but at the beginning of the example, I mentioned that the computer had a maximum of 2 GB. Because of this, that would most likely not work because the computer can only recognize a maximum of 2 GB, which would probably be 1 GB in each slot. Nothing too complicated, but you just want to be aware of things like this when buying a new computer or adding more memory to your computer.

How much am I using?

One important question that you may be wondering is how much RAM you are using. To find this out in the Windows Vista operating system, you will want to do the following:

> • <u>Right-click</u> on an open area of the taskbar along the bottom and select "Task Manager."

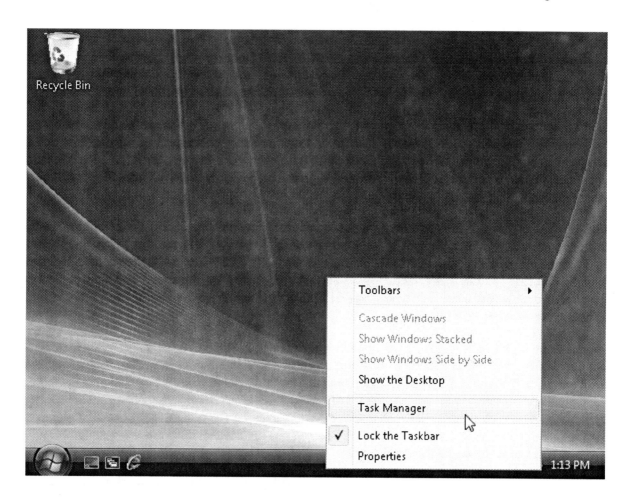

> • When the "Task Manager" comes up, go to the "Performance" tab.

• Here's a better idea of some of the important numbers you'll find here:
1. *Physical Memory (MB)* - Total - This number tells you how much RAM is actually installed on your computer. In the case of the screenshot shown next, you'll see this computer has 1023 MB installed, which is approximately 1 GB. Remember that there are 1,024 MB in 1 GB. So 1,023 MB / 1,024 = 0.9990234375 GB.

2. *Physical Memory (MB)* - Cached - This refers to the amount of memory that the system has recently used for system resources. Windows Vista has a new feature called "Windows SuperFetch™" memory management. It runs in the background to determine which applications you use most and puts them into most of the unused RAM to help speed those applications up for you. That is what the cached memory is that you see here.

3. *Physical Memory (MB)* - Free - This is the amount of memory that is unused at this point in time. In this case, this computer has about 10 MB free.

4. *Page File* - This is an important couple of numbers. They are there to tell you about the page file (also known as virtual memory). When the computer runs out of physical installed RAM to use, it writes to and reads the information to the hard drive on a file called the page file. Unfortunately, using the mechanical hard drive is much slower than using electronic RAM. The first number shows the amount of installed RAM and virtual memory (the page file) that is in use at this point in time. The second number is the total amount of installed RAM combined with the size of the virtual memory available.

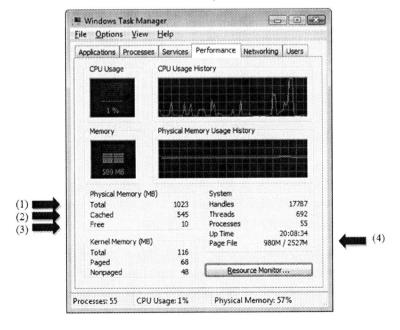

So, what does this tell you? The first number in the page file information is probably the most important. In this example, I am using a total of 980 MB. We already determined that I have 1,023 MB of installed RAM. The key is that if the 980 MB of memory in use were to increase to above 1,023, it means the Windows Vista OS has started to use the page file because it has no more installed RAM left. And that also means your computer will likely slow to a crawl because of how slow page file access is.

In this example, there are really no major applications open right now. About half the RAM is being used by the Windows Vista OS as well as applications running in the background. If I start opening a few software programs, such as the Microsoft Outlook email client, the Internet Explorer browser, and the Quicken software, suddenly the first number for the "Page File" jumps up to 1,081 MB.

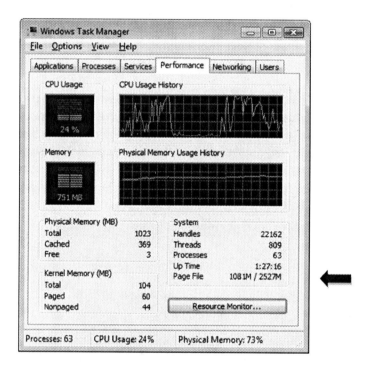

1,081 MB is more than the 1,023 MB of installed RAM and has drastically slowed down the computer. This is a sign that this computer needs more physical RAM. If you usually keep a few software applications open at the same time, you will probably run into this same problem.

I generally would recommend that you have no less than 1 GB (1,024 MB) of physical RAM installed on a computer running Windows Vista. If possible, however, I would suggest beefing this up to 2 GB (2,048 MB). Trust me - you'll thank me later! RAM is one of the least expensive, but most effective performance boosters you can give your computer.

chapter 4

CPUs (Processors)

What are they?

For most end users, when you buy a new computer, you should be able to get up to 5 years of useful life out of it. Any more than that and you'll probably want to throw it out the window because of how slow it will be. In any case, unless you are a techie that understands computer hardware, chances are the most you might do with a computer's hardware over its lifetime is adding more memory.

Typical users don't try to rebuild a computer to get better performance out of it. It's true that after a few years you could replace the CPU, also known as the processor, on your computer to give you a little more boost. However, unless you know what you're doing and where to shop, the cost and effort of doing that is unlikely to be justifiable. A very basic new computer can be purchased for around $300. A new processor will likely run you a couple hundred dollars. With that in mind, as well as the fact that replacing the processor will still leave you with a computer that is likely out of warranty, the idea of getting a new computer may be a more viable option.

That being said, there are a couple technologies that stand out in the world of processors that you should be aware of - 64-bit computing and multi-core processors.

64-bit computing

Currently, the majority of PCs are 32-bit. This refers to the number of bits that can be processed at the same time by the processor. I won't delve into the technical details, but 32-bit architectures have their limitations, such as only being able to work with four gigabytes of RAM.

64-bit processors can handle 64 bits in parallel. It can also support up to a terabyte of RAM (1000 GB). 64-bit computing has been around for years, but has been used mainly by technologies such as supercomputing and extremely large database systems. It has recently begun to become more prominent in the industry due to availability in operating systems (such as Windows), desktop software, and hardware drivers.

The reason this is important to know is that you will start to find that you now have a choice when buying a new computer. You can go with a 32-bit system or a 64-bit system. Years from now, 32-bit systems will become obsolete. However, for almost all home or home office users, 32-bit computers should be just fine over the next couple of years. Much of the use of PCs is for web browsing, running word processing or spreadsheet applications, and email. These are tasks that do not have much to gain from a 64-bit system. The flow of 64-bit computing will likely gain more traction in the server world and then begin to trickle down to desktops and notebooks. While that is happening, more and more software will become available for 64-bit systems. So for now, unless you are working with software such as computer-aided design (CAD), performing a lot of video encoding, or are a big gamer, 64-bit systems will not offer you too much to gain to justify the price difference.

Multi-core processors

The other technology you should be aware of is multi-core processors. As CPU manufacturers (such as Intel and AMD) took the speed of single processors to their physical limits, they needed something to allow for continued ingenuity to help with sales and the growth of the industry. What was developed was a way to put more than one processor on the same integrated circuit. This allowed for better performance, more efficient handling of multiple tasks, and reduced power consumption. In general, a dual core processor (two processors on the same integrated circuit) will likely give about a 50% performance increase over a single processor. The dual core is the current processor showing up in new computers. Over time, you will begin to see even more processors on a single integrated circuit - quad-core, eight-core, or even more.

Multi-core processors are important to know about simply because of the performance gains you can obtain. In general, you will start to notice that almost all new computers will begin to have multi-core processors, but you should be aware of this, so you can decide what makes sense for you. When looking at buying a new computer, you may be thinking that a new single processor computer may be much better than the single processor computer you have right now. However, a couple years from now, you may find yourself wishing you had gone with the computer with a multi-core processor.

Most of the time, you will not need to spend too much time thinking about the processors offered. New computers will likely be offered with the newest processor technologies available and unless you are planning to do more intensive computing, you should be just fine with the speed and type you see on most advertised computers.

III. The Basics of Wireless

chapter 5

Wireless

A brief history

Home wireless networking has become increasingly popular - almost commonplace - and rightly so. This allows many home users and small businesses to be able to connect to the Internet or start a home network without the need to run cabling through difficult and sometimes nearly impossible locations.

Keep in mind that the wireless technology we're talking about here is known as WLAN, or wireless local area networks. It is generally used for homes and businesses mainly for relatively short distances, similar to cordless phones. Other technologies like cell phones and satellites are something of a completely different nature.

As the popularity for these WLAN technologies has increased, the standards have begun to evolve. When wireless functionality started to be tested in places, there were a couple choices - 802.11a and 802.11b.

802.11b operates over the airwaves on the 2.4 GHz (gigahertz) frequency. This might sound familiar because until recently, most cordless phones also use the 2.4 GHz frequency. Not by coincidence, cordless phones that operate in this frequency can cause interference with 802.11b wireless networks. Putting an 802.11b wireless device next to many microwaves can also cause interference.

802.11b also offers speeds of up to 11 Mbps (megabits per second). This means that it can accommodate downloading or transferring files at a maximum of 11 Mbps. However, most broadband cable connections to the Internet (a faster option than dial-up or DSL) will generally give you speeds of only around 1.5 Mbps for downloads. This is what's called a bottleneck. Even though your wireless connection can accommodate up to 11 Mbps, if the cable connection is giving you only 1.5 Mbps, that's the maximum you'll get when accessing the Internet. For most home users though, this speed is plenty.

As a side note, you will generally be able to take advantage of that 11 Mbps speed if you're transferring files between two computers on the same network. Let's say you have two computers at home both connecting to a wireless 802.11b device for instance, you should be able to copy an extremely large file from one to the other in a short amount of time. The final point to make about the 802.11b standard is that it usually provides a range of around 100 to 150 feet indoors, depending on how the rooms are set up, the type of construction, etc. This is actually not too bad, and if one wireless router is put in the right location, it can generally accommodate wireless devices throughout most of a house.

802.11a provides for some different options. It operates on the 5 GHz frequency. This frequency is considered less crowded than the 2.4 GHz band because of the lack of devices on it. Less crowded means less interference on a network. Recently, however, more cordless phones are being manufactured to use the 5 GHz range.

802.11a offers speeds of up to 54 Mbps! This is about five times the speed offered by the 802.11b standard! Remember though - you can only get up to the maximum speed of the slowest link. So if you have DSL that offers speeds of 768 Kbps (about half of what you got with the cable connection), then 768 Kbps is also the maximum speed you can get on a download over your wireless connection. That means much of the speed you're offered will not be able to be taken advantage of anyway.

802.11a provides a range of around 25 to 75 feet indoors, again dependent of the structure of the building, walls, etc. This is much less than what the 802.11b standard has to offer.

So users were forced to make choices. If they chose 802.11b, they got the better range of distance, but a slower speed and possibly interference with things such as cordless phones. If they went with 802.11a, they got better potential speed offerings and less possibility of interference, but also less range.

A little later, in the early 2000s, a new standard became available... 802.11g. 802.11g sought to combine the best of both 802.11a and 802.11b. It supports up to 54 Mbps, uses the 2.4 GHz frequency, which lets it provide backward compatibility to support the 802.11b standard, and provides for a distance range of around 100 to 150 feet. 802.11g has now quickly become the predominant wireless technology for homes and small businesses.

The following table provides a summary of the 802.11 WLAN standards.

Wireless Standards Comparison Table

	802.11a	802.11b	802.11g
Speed	Up to 54 Mbps	Up to 11 Mbps	Up to 54 Mbps
Frequency	5 GHz band	2.4 GHz band	2.4 GHz band
Range	Generally 25 to 75 feet indoors	Generally 100 to 150 feet indoors	Generally 100 to 150 feet indoors
Compatibility	Incompatible with both 802.11b and 802.11g	Can be used in 802.11g networks	Backward compatible with 802.11b devices

Here and now

802.11g wireless devices have become extremely popular and the price has dramatically dropped for almost all of these devices. To help keep their profits up, these WLAN device makers have added their own technologies to the standards... "802.11g with speed enhancer." The products that come out with technologies such as these usually provide what they say, but they come with a problem as well.

The problem is that they usually only work with other products made by the same vendor. Standards are created to be able to provide interoperability. If you have an 802.11g router made by one company, you should be able to connect to it using wireless technology by any other device even by another manufacturer, as long as they support the 802.11g standard. The "additional functionality" provided by these manufacturers trap you into using only their products. If you want to gain the additional functionality promised by the router, you need to have a network card by the same vendor to support this. If you have a laptop that came with integrated wireless built into it (which almost all new ones do today), it will likely be able to connect as an 802.11g device. However, it will probably not be able to take advantage of this speed enhancer. To do that, you will need to shell out some dollars for a wireless network card made by the vendor that supports the speed enhancer. And because it has these super-duper powers built into it, the price is usually higher than a standard 802.11g router. Why spend the extra money when wireless is already built in? As discussed earlier, you will probably not be able to take advantage of the speed when downloading anyway due to the bottleneck of the speed you get from your ISP for cable or DSL.

A new draft standard, 802.11n, was approved by the IEEE 802.11n Working Group standards committee on January 19, 2006. 802.11n builds upon the former 802.11 standards by adding MIMO or Multiple Input Multiple Output. This takes advantage of multiple antennas to provide a much higher data throughput. 802.11n promises speeds of up to 540 Mbps (almost 10 times faster than 802.11g!). This helps make 802.11n a strong contender for more business networks. Currently, the majority of wired networks allow for speeds of 100 Mbps up to 1 Gbps of shared throughput for users. 802.11n will provide a nice middle ground for these networks. It is not likely to see many devices supporting the 802.11n standard until the end of 2007. However, there are already some "Pre-N" devices on the market. These devices are based around what the standard will "likely" be and are not guaranteed to be compatible once the standard is complete. I recommend getting an 802.11g router for now and sticking with that until the fully certified 802.11n devices officially come out.

What do I need?

So, now that you have a basic understanding of some of the technology, you might be asking, "What do I need to get this set up?" Well, you'll probably be surprised at just how simple and relatively inexpensive it is to do. In most cases, all you'll need is a wireless router and maybe a wireless network adapter.

If you have a newer laptop, it may very well have wireless already built into it. You'll need to find out what standards it supports. Read this in the documentation or you can check in Device Manager by doing the following:

1) Open Device Manager:

- In the Windows Vista OS, if you *are* an administrator, click on the "Start" button and in the search box (which can also act similar to the "Run" button that previous Windows operating systems used), type in **devmgmt.msc**, and then press the "ENTER" key. If prompted for permission, click "Continue."

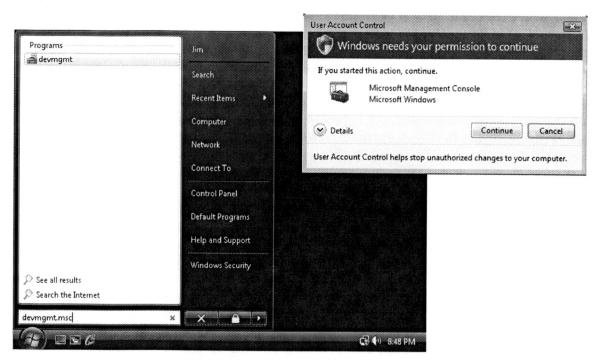

- In the Windows Vista OS, if you are *not* an administrator, click on the "Start" button and in the search box (which can also act similar to the "Run" button that previous Windows operating systems used), type in **devmgmt.msc**, <u>right-click</u> on "devmgmt.msc" in the search results and choose "Run as administrator." Enter in the password for an administrator account.

2) Once the "Device Manager" opens, expand out "Network Adapters" by clicking on the plus sign and look for an adapter that might be a wireless giveaway. In the case of my laptop (running the Windows Vista OS), my wireless adapter is called "Intel(R) PRO/Wireless 2200BG Network Connection."

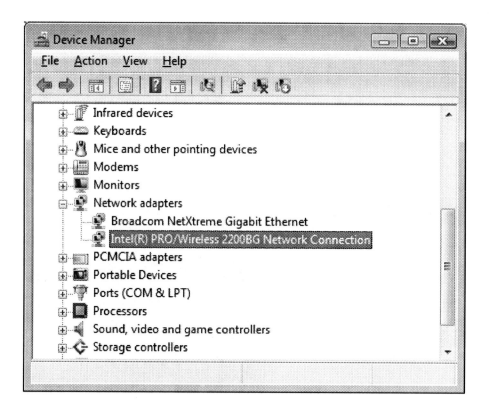

3) If you don't see anything listed as wireless here, you'll probably need to get a wireless network card for your laptop.

Many broadband ISPs (Internet Service Providers) are now giving users wireless routers to use when they sign up for the duration of their service. If you recently signed up for DSL or cable Internet, you may have already gotten most of the way there. If not, it shouldn't be too big of a deal. As of this writing, you can pick up an 802.11g router (no non-standard speed enhancement abilities) with a built in 4-port switch for around $50 after rebates.

Head up to a store like Wal-Mart, Best Buy, or Circuit City and go to the section with wireless networking equipment. If you don't already have anything in place using earlier technologies such as 802.11a or 802.11b, I would recommend getting an 802.11g router. If by the time you're reading this the 802.11n products are officially out and in your price range, then go with one of those. What you want is a router labeled as an 802.11g (or 802.11n) router. Some of the big names right now are Linksys, NETGEAR, D-Link, and Belkin®. Personally, I like the Linksys products because they are now owned by Cisco, a very solid and trusted networking company, but any of them should do fine. Most wireless routers now have a small switch with maybe four ports built right into them. This would be used if you have a computer that won't be connected wirelessly. Maybe you have a laptop that will connect wirelessly as well as a desktop computer that you don't want to buy a wireless network adapter for. The switch allows you to connect the desktop computer directly to it with a standard network cable, called an Ethernet cable.

If you determined that you also need a wireless network adapter for your computer then you'll want to get this as well. I would recommend sticking with the same vendor - i.e. if you're getting a Linksys router, get a Linksys network adapter. Mixed vendor products should work together as long as they followed the same wireless standard, but that doesn't always happen. You'll probably save yourself a headache by sticking with the same manufacturer.

Wireless laptop cards and wireless desktop cards are not usually going to be the same product. If you have a laptop, the wireless network card will probably be a PCMCIA card. Don't worry about the acronym; just know that the card is for the slot(s) on your laptop that are usually about a couple inches wide. Most newer laptops can accommodate any of the three types of PCMCIA cards. If you have a desktop computer, the wireless card will likely be a PCI card. Again, the acronym isn't important, but on a desktop computer, it's one of usually a couple of slots on the back of the computer that will be covered with a piece of metal about a few inches long and about an inch wide. The cover is taken off, the metal slot cover taken off and the new card inserted. When buying a wireless card, just be sure it supports the same standard as the router - i.e. 802.11g or 802.11n.

You will probably start to see more wireless cards begin to shift toward USB. The same information as above will still apply with these, except that installation is all but eliminated - just plug and play!

Once you have your new router and your wireless card (if needed), follow the manufacturer's instructions to get everything set up. If possible, you'll want to set up the router in a central location to be able to get the best signal, regardless of where you are in the house (or office). The manufacturer should include drawings to show you how to piece things together, but here is picture showing a probable layout...

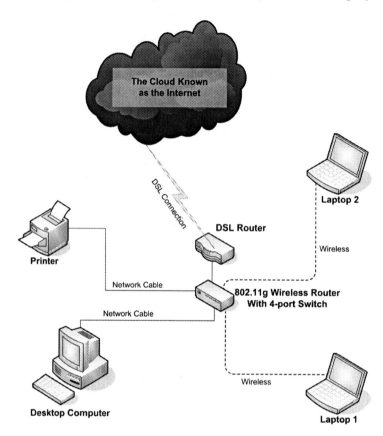

And that's it. You should now be able to get out to the Internet without the need to be directly connected with a cable to your router. If you have a laptop that you move around the house, you'll soon learn if you have any spots where the wireless connection is not very strong. You can avoid those places in the house, move the router to a different location, or get a wireless repeater from the store to help alleviate this.

Security

When wireless local area networks (WLANs) first started to hit the market, one of the biggest concerns was security. If an attacker who knew what they were doing (also known as a hacker) was to be in an area where they could access your wireless connection - say, sitting in their car on the street in front of your house or office - he could potentially see any data that is transmitted through the air. This means your email could be read and possibly user names and passwords could be stolen.

In an attempt to thwart these security issues, Wired Equivalent Privacy (WEP) was developed with the 802.11b standard. However, WEP was soon learned to have security weaknesses and was not as secure as originally thought. This caused a great concern for any hopes of wireless to continue to grow.

To help alleviate some of these concerns, a new security standard called Wi-Fi Protected Access (WPA) was created. WPA brought a certain sense of relief to the industry's security concerns. WPA includes the ability to use the Temporal Key Integrity Protocol (TKIP) protocol to encrypt data. This allowed for several security features that were not available with WEP. One of these is key mixing, which gives a hacker less data to work with off one security key, making it a much more complex process for any potential attacker. TKIP also provides WPA with a message integrity checking ability to help stop the wireless data from being forged. Additionally, WEP had allowed an important piece of data called the initialization vector (IV) to be sent in plain text. If this were to be attained, it could allow an attacker to decrypt the data without ever needing the password. This was one of WEP's biggest vulnerabilities. WPA with TKIP fixes this by taking the IV and encrypting it using RC4 and by hashing it.

Wi-Fi Protected Access 2 (WPA2) soon came out as the successor to WPA. WPA2 provides network access control and stronger data protection. It was based on the IEEE 802.11i standard and allowed for Advanced Encryption Standard (AES), a government-adopted security standard. It came out in two versions, WPA2-Personal (meant for home and small businesses) and WPA2-Enterprise (which is used with authentication through a network server). WPA2 is also backward compatible with WPA. This means if you have a wireless router set up to use WPA2 and one of the computers connecting to it only supports WPA, the wireless router can still accommodate that computer. That user however does not gain the additional benefits of WPA2.

Now we have to decide what method of security should be set up on your wireless network...

In order of security from best to worst, you have the following:
- WPA2
- WPA
- WEP
- No security

Here's a good rule of thumb - use the highest security that is supported by both your wireless router and your computer(s). Older wireless routers may only support WEP. You may be able to upgrade the firmware on an older router to be able to support WPA, however. All new wireless routers should support WPA2.

Support for WPA2 in the Windows operating system was released for the Windows XP OS in May of 2005. This is for computers that are running the Windows XP OS with a minimum of Service Pack 2 (see **http://support.microsoft.com/?id=893357** for more information). If you are running the Windows Vista OS, built-in support for WPA2 is included right out of the box!

If you have a computer with a version of the Windows operating system older than the Windows XP OS, built-in support for WPA2 is not available. However, it is likely that the manufacturer of any new wireless adapter that you have or get for the computer has software or a software update that provides WPA2 support.

If you cannot use WPA2, I would strongly recommend at least setting up WPA for a little peace of mind. If you are however set up to use WPA2, you can feel confident that as of now, the encryption has not been cracked and only authorized users can access your wireless network.

Here are some other security tips I would recommend. Please keep in mind that while some of these can be argued that they will not keep your wireless network 100% secure, they will however make it more difficult for an attacker to compromise the network. While any network can be compromised given enough time and resources, our hope is that an attacker will move on to a less secure network instead of wasting time on yours.

- **Change the default SSID and turn off broadcasting** - The SSID is the Service Set Identifier. It is the name your computer uses to connect to the wireless router. It's basically an identifier. So if you set up the SSID on the router to be MyWirelessLAN, then in order for a device such as your computer to be able to connect to it, it needs to know what to connect to. In this instance then, the wireless card needs to know to connect to MyWirelessLAN.

  The problem is that when most wireless routers are set up using the defaults, the defaults are usually to broadcast the SSID. This means that your wireless card will search for wireless SSIDs being broadcast to let you easily connect to it. It also means it's out there letting an attacker know that there is a wireless network nearby and he or she has already become one step closer to compromising your network. Granted, an SSID can be found out otherwise, but remember, our objective is just to make things difficult for the attacker.

  If you purchase a Linksys router for instance, it has a default SSID of linksys. If an attacker were to see that SSID being broadcast, he or she would now know what kind of device it is (including any vulnerabilities it may have) and will assume that you set up the router using the defaults. This means he or she has more knowledge than you would like them to have. They now also may want to see if you left the administrator password of the device at the default as well!

  So give a quick check through the manual of the wireless router and find out how to change the default SSID to something different and obscure. Then find out how to turn off the SSID broadcast feature on the router as well.

- **Change the default Administrator credentials** - One of the first things you should do is change the default Administrator password on the wireless router. You, as well as any attacker, can easily find out the default password for a wireless device by simply doing a quick search on the Internet. Change this password immediately to something obscure (and not the same as that password you have for everything else that requires one!). If the device allows it, I would also change the user name as well. Every attacker knows that almost all the time, the administrative user name of a device is either administrator or admin. With that, they are now 50% done solving the equation. The only other piece they need is the password. Change the user name to something - anything else... how about calling it theboss or yourmajesty?

- **Enable MAC address filtering** - Every network adapter (the card in the computer that lets you connect to a network) has a unique identifier embedded in it - kind of like a serial number. This is called its Media Access Control (MAC) address. This address actually travels alongside the data that moves across a network.

You can use the MAC address to help address security as well. On your wireless router, you will most likely have an option to perform what is called MAC filtering. You'll have to check the manual to know how to set it, but for the most part, what it does is gives you the ability to tell the router let only the MAC addresses of the computers you want to be able to use the router. All other packets of data will then be dropped by the router. So how do you find your computer's MAC address?

> o Click on the "Start" button and in the search box, type in **cmd**, and then press the "ENTER" key.

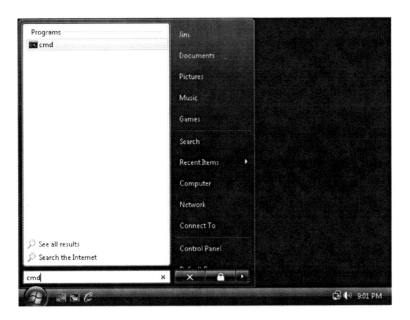

In the command prompt that comes up, type in **ipconfig /all** and then hit the Enter key. Find the section on your wireless network connection and look for where it says "Physical Address." The twelve-digit string of numbers with hyphens between every two numbers is the MAC address for that network adapter. I've done a little editing to make mine all zeroes for security reasons, but that's where you'll find it.

```
Select Administrator: Command Prompt                          _ □ ×

C:\>ipconfig /all

Windows IP Configuration

    Host Name . . . . . . . . . . . . : JJ
    Primary Dns Suffix  . . . . . . . : bpi.local
    Node Type . . . . . . . . . . . . : Hybrid
    IP Routing Enabled. . . . . . . . : No
    WINS Proxy Enabled. . . . . . . . : No
    DNS Suffix Search List. . . . . . : bpi.local
                                        neo.rr.com

Wireless LAN adapter Wireless Network Connection:

    Connection-specific DNS Suffix  . : neo.rr.com
    Description . . . . . . . . . . . : Intel(R) PRO/Wireless 2200BG Network Conn
ection
    Physical Address. . . . . . . . . : 00-00-00-00-00-00
    DHCP Enabled. . . . . . . . . . . : Yes
    Autoconfiguration Enabled . . . . : Yes
    Link-local IPv6 Address . . . . . : fe80::70d3:c364:a2c7:ce69%9(Preferred)
    IPv4 Address. . . . . . . . . . . : 192.168.1.102(Preferred)
    Subnet Mask . . . . . . . . . . . : 255.255.255.0
    Lease Obtained. . . . . . . . . . : Tuesday, December 26, 2006 9:36:55 AM
```

This is the number you want to jot down to add to the "allowed" MAC addresses on your wireless router. Any computer you want to be able to connect to the router will also need its MAC address added as well.

An attacker can use certain programs to allow them to "spoof" their MAC address so it looks like another, but that involves quite a bit more effort seeing as they must first do some work to "sniff" the network traffic to find an allowed MAC address (yours). Once again, we simply want to deter any malicious activity - it's never possible to make it 100% foolproof.

Troubleshooting tip

I just want to share a quick tip with you before ending this chapter. When I first installed my wireless router, I was excited to be able to set up my laptop wherever I wanted in the house and still get access to the Internet. However, I noticed that whenever anyone would use the cordless phone and walk somewhere between the path of my laptop and the router, my connection to the Internet would drop.

As I mentioned earlier, this is because both my wireless connection and the cordless phone both used the 2.4 GHz frequency. Here's all I had to do to alleviate this problem...

The 2.4 GHz frequency is broken down into smaller bands called channels. You probably have used or seen the "channel" button on cordless phones that when pressed, goes to a channel with less interference. You also have the option to change the channel in the wireless world. The default channel for many wireless routers is 6, but this can be changed fairly quickly in most cases. You can go into the administration or configuration of the router (usually just a webpage - check the instructions for how to get to it) and simply change the channel it uses. In the United States for example, the options should be channels 1 through 11 - these are the permitted channels allowed.

A quick 2 minute fix, but once I made the change on my router, the problem was no longer a problem. This can also fix problems where you might lose your wireless connection due to another wireless device using the same channel, such as a neighbor's wireless router.

IV. The Basics of Operating Systems

chapter 6

Operating Systems

The operating system is arguably the most important part of any computer. The operating system takes care of what most people would consider basic tasks, such as taking in input from devices (the keyboard, mouse, etc.) and outputting to the monitor. It is also responsible for keeping track of files and controlling devices such as printers and USB drives. It is often compared to a traffic cop in that it is in charge of making sure that programs don't interfere with each other.

Operating systems have evolved tremendously over the years of computers. I don't think a history lesson is pertinent to what you are probably seeking from this book, so please just know that although the Microsoft Windows is probably the most well known operating system, it is certainly not the only fish in the sea. Macintosh ("Mac") is an operating system that has been around for just about the same length of time as the Windows OS. Many professionals in the world of art or music would never consider anything but a Mac computer. You may have also heard of the Linux operating system, which is promising to take over as the alternative to the Windows OS. There are many others out there, but our focus is on the market leader and most recognized operating system - Windows.

The Microsoft Windows OS has definitely grown up since its days starting out in the early eighties. Although it is run by the majority of computer users, Microsoft has had many stumbling blocks learning the ropes. Windows 95, the first of its 32-bit operating systems was impressive in its day, but was still immature and did not have much of the stability you find now. Security problems have always plagued Microsoft and could have eventually caused a downfall of the company's biggest moneymaker. However, the times have changed, Microsoft has learned through its own mistakes and the mistakes of others and they are slowly winning back the confidence of even some of its worst critics.

Anyone running any of the newer Microsoft operating systems - Windows 2000 (released in 2000), Windows XP (released in 2001), and its newest flagship Windows Vista (released in 2006/2007) are all solid products. With each new operating system, security has become more of a focus as well as stability.

chapter 7

Windows XP

As of this writing, the Windows XP OS is the most predominant operating system from Microsoft. However, in the computer world, it's becoming an old man. It was released in late 2001. The newest operating system (OS) from Microsoft, Windows Vista, will likely take some time to build up to the popularity of the Windows XP OS.

The Windows XP operating system has proved to be a very stable. Stability was something you never really found in the early versions of the Windows OS - all too common was what is commonly referred to as the "Blue Screen of Death" (BSOD). You might be working in the Windows operating sytem and then suddenly, a dark blue screen would come up with white lettering, telling you that a problem occurred. This generally happens when the Windows OS encounters a problem from which it can't recover. Here's a sample screenshot of what a "Blue Screen" might look like...

```
A problem has been detected and windows has been shut down to prevent damage
to your computer.

The end-user manually generated the crashdump.

If this is the first time you've seen this Stop error screen,
restart your computer. If this screen appears again, follow
these steps:

Check to make sure any new hardware or software is properly installed.
If this is a new installation, ask your hardware or software manufacturer
for any Windows updates you might need.

If problems continue, disable or remove any newly installed hardware
or software. Disable BIOS memory options such as caching or shadowing.
If you need to use Safe Mode to remove or disable components, restart
your computer, press F8 to select Advanced Startup Options, and then
select Safe Mode.

Technical information:

*** STOP: 0x000000E2 (0x00000000,0x00000000,0x00000000,0x00000000)


Beginning dump of physical memory
Dumping physical memory to disk:  33
```

At that point, either your computer restarts automatically or you need to physically power it off and turn it back on. Neither is very nice because if you had any unsaved data on the computer (like an open, unsaved Word document), you would lose it. This used to be a relatively common occurrence in earlier versions of the Windows operating system, but starting with the Windows 2000 OS (the version before Windows XP), this became a less frequent event. It still happens periodically, but definitely not as much in the Windows XP OS.

The Windows XP operating system also incorporated a much-needed security overhaul with the introduction of Service Pack 2. This included things such as the Windows Firewall, a pop-up blocker for the Internet Explorer browser, and many extremely important changes to the operating system internally. I won't go into details on the internal changes, but you can always go to **http://www.microsoft.com/windowsxp/sp2/default.mspx** for more information. If you're running the Windows XP OS, make sure you have this Service Pack installed at minimum (Service Pack 3 is expected to be released in 2008). You can go to **http://update.microsoft.com** to see if it is available for you... if not, then you're already covered. If it is available, make sure to download it from here and install it because this is an extremely important security update.

Because the Windows XP OS is soon to be replaced, I won't spend too much time discussing all the details about it. In fact, more than likely, if you've bought a new computer since it was released in 2001, you've probably been using it. Here's a brief summary of some of the other features that Windows XP brought to the table...

- Speedier boot-up - Previous versions of the Windows OS took quite some time to start up and get loaded. The Windows XP OS included a new boot sequence that helped speed things up.

- Remote Desktop - In the Professional Edition of the Windows XP operating system, a feature called Remote Desktop is included that allows you to work on your computer from a remote location anywhere in the world. Although a fantastic feature, most home or home-office users don't take advantage of this because either they are unaware that it exists or they don't know how to make the necessary changes on their Internet router or firewall. As a side note, to set this feature up so your computer can be reached from out on the Internet, TCP port 3389 needs to be opened up to your computer (some more information can currently be found at: **http://www.microsoft.com/windowsxp/using/mobility/rdfaq.mspx).**

- Built-in wireless - In earlier versions of the Windows operating system, you had to have third-party wireless software in order to use wireless on your computer. The Windows XP OS added built-in, native support for wireless and made configuration even easier with Service Pack 2. Although wireless vendors normally include software to use with their wireless products, the built-in Windows capabilities can generally be used instead. Keep in mind you need to have wireless hardware added or built-in to your computer to be able to do any wireless connectivity.

- Driver rollback - Drivers are software that tells the Windows OS how to communicate to and use hardware. So, if you added a new wireless card to your computer for instance, the manufacturer of the card would include software with a driver to be installed. The driver then gives the Windows operating system all the information it needs to be able to use the wireless card. Sometimes the manufacturer's drivers are not well written and can cause problems with the operating system (like the "Blue Screen of Death"). Microsoft has become stricter on how it wants drivers to be written, but problems still do happen. In earlier versions of the Windows OS, if you had a bad driver that was installed, it could essentially make the operating system unusable. If you couldn't remove the bad driver, you might get to the point you would actually need to reinstall the Windows OS. The Windows XP operating system includes a feature to "roll back" the driver to the previous version to help prevent this from happening.

- Fast user switching - If Dennis is logged on and has a number of programs open and Kevin comes over and needs to check his email, Kevin can switch over to his own desktop and account without Dennis needing to close out of everything and log off first. When Kevin is done, Dennis can go right back over to his desktop and resume all his open programs. This functionality is new in Windows XP.

- New interface - The interface was revamped and made into a more "user-friendly" design.

At this point in time, most users are probably familiar with the basics of the Windows XP operating system. Additionally if you're getting a new computer, you may not even need to be since most new computers will come with the Windows Vista OS pre-installed.

chapter 8

Windows Vista

Windows Vista is the newest operating system from Microsoft. As always, with any new operating system, Microsoft will tell you that this is the "solve-all" to all your problems. Well, that's up to you to decide. I will tell you, however, that Microsoft has done something with this operating system (OS) that it has never done before... it's building the operating system around security rather than adding security to an already complete operating system. This is an extremely important step in the right direction for Microsoft. It is always better to have security as your focus from the start rather than trying to conform one thing into something else.

For instance, with previous Microsoft operating systems, in order to be able to run applications without running into problems, the majority of people use a user account that is an administrator of the local computer. When logged on with an account that is a member of the Administrators group, you now have full reign to do whatever you desire on the computer. Convenience comes at a steep price though, because in addition to you having full reign on the computer, so do any programs that are running while you are logged on... including viruses, spyware, and other malware. A virus now has the power to delete everything on your computer. Wouldn't it make more sense for a user to have limited rights and then if higher access was needed to do something, let the user know and allow them to type in a password to get access for that one-time event?

Of course it would! In fact, many operating systems such as Linux have been doing this for years. Well, Microsoft has now decided to get on the ball. The Windows Vista operating system now offers what they are referring to as User Account Control. When you want to do something that requires administrative rights, you'll be prompted to allow it to run or be asked for a password...

It will definitely take some getting used to for all of us that had the power to accomplish tasks without the hassle of a popup box asking us for a password all the time. That's certainly true, but if you've ever gotten a bad virus or spyware, you know how much hassle it can be to have it removed or in many cases, needing to reload the entire operating system. Additionally, everyday tasks like working with Word or Excel software, browsing the Internet, or checking email will most likely not give you this prompt. The prompt will occur, however, if you are installing a new application, for example.

The Windows Vista OS adds other features that are likely to be a big hit with users. Here are some of the highlights:

- **User experience** - One of big pushes from Microsoft is the "user experience." The idea is that everything will be much easier to organize, find, and work with.

    o **Desktop search** - An integrated search function is now scattered throughout the Windows Vista OS. You may have used the search function in previous versions of the Windows operating system and notice it takes a while for it to find your document(s) - if it even finds it. The desktop search eliminates many of these headaches. It works by indexing files, including content from most files. This means you don't necessarily need to remember the name of the file, but maybe a word or words from within a document, the name of the artist for a song file, etc. And once you punch in what you're looking for, the results instantly pop up because they've already been indexed. No more waiting.

    o **Preview panes and thumbnails** - When looking at a folder of files, you can now click once on a file and see a live preview of the content inside, rather than opening each file to find the one you want. When resting your mouse over an item along the taskbar, you'll see a live thumbnail (a small preview) of what that window contains.

- **Security** - We already discussed User Account Control, what I consider to be one of the most important features of Windows Vista. Here are a couple others...

    o Windows Defender - Now built into the Windows Vista OS, Microsoft has added an anti-spyware utility to monitor for problems such as spyware or other unwanted software.

    o Firewall - Windows XP was the first version of the Windows operating system to come out with a software firewall built into it. The problem was that it only worked to take care of connections that were inbound to the computer. The Windows Vista OS now has a firewall that can protect both inbound and outbound connections to the computer. We will discuss what firewalls do and their importance more in the section "The Basics of Protecting Your Computer."

- **Internet Explorer 7** - Microsoft hasn't really done much with their web browser until recently. For quite some time, Microsoft owned almost the entire market with its Internet Explorer browser. Then, the Mozilla® Foundation came out with an Internet browser called Firefox® that has taken the market by storm. According to SpreadFirefox (a non-profit organization set to help market Firefox), as of March 2006, Firefox has had more than 150 million downloads! At that point, Microsoft decided to get back to work on its Internet Explorer web browser. The Internet Explorer 7 browser, included with the Windows Vista OS and downloadable for the Windows XP OS, has incorporated some really nice features. One of these is tabbed browsing, a feature that was already built into the Firefox browser and many other web browsers. Tabbed browsing is just a way of using tabs from within your main

67

browser window to have multiple sites open at the same time instead several windows that can quickly fill the taskbar. Security was also taken into consideration, limiting the Internet Explorer browser to just being able to browse the web, as it should be.

- **Sleep** - A new power feature called Sleep has been introduced. If you are a fan of Standby or Hibernate, then you will probably be very interested in the Sleep feature. It combines the best of both worlds, giving you the speed of going to Standby and the low energy use of Hibernate. In a nutshell, this is something more often to be used by laptop users than desktop users. Essentially, when you hit the power button or close the lid of your laptop, all the applications and data that are currently open and running are written to memory. When you turn on the laptop, in just a couple seconds, you are right back to where you left off (open documents and all) with no need to wait for the computer to start up. If for some reason, it takes you longer than expected to get back to your laptop and the Windows Vista operating system sees the battery life getting low, the data will be written from memory to the hard drive.

- **SuperFetch** - A new technology by Microsoft that learns which applications you use most and "preloads" those applications into memory so when you go to use one of those applications, it will load much faster.

- **Backing Up** - This is another item that we will discuss more later on in the book. The Windows Vista operating system makes a couple of improvements on backups.

  o System Restore - If you've needed to use the System Restore feature in the Windows XP OS, you know just how important this feature is. System Restore is a technology that the Windows operating system uses to take snapshot backups of your system on a regular basis. Sometimes something can cause major problems, such as a virus or application, to the point you're about ready to throw the computer out the window. System Restore is an option that will lets the Windows operating system be rolled back to the way it was at a previous time (hopefully before the problem occurred). The Windows Vista OS improves upon the technology that was released with the Windows XP OS.

  o Backup - In previous Windows operating system versions, the backup utility lacked some major functionality. Although it would do a good job doing the backups and restores of data, it did not allow you to back up directly to CDs, DVDs, or external hard drives (USB or FireWire®). This made backups a bit more troublesome for the typical home user. If you wanted to back up data to a CD or DVD, you had to back up the computer to itself (or another computer). Then if you wanted, you could move the backup file to another location off the computer (like burning it to a DVD). Where's the automation in that?! Well, now there's no excuse for users not to have a backup run on a regular basis. The ability to back up to external devices is now built in. We'll talk more about getting this set up in the section "The Basics of Backups."

o Volume Shadow Copies - Have you ever accidentally been working with a file and you don't want to save any changes, but when you are prompted if you want to save your changes, you jump the gun and click "Yes" and write over things you didn't want to be changed? Well, Microsoft has now included a technology it had originally used in its Windows Server™ 2003 product line that will automatically create snapshots of files at certain times of the day. If you need a file back, you can easily look for and most likely see multiple versions of the file that exist. Then you can save the version of the file back to its original location or to another location if desired.

- **Parental Controls** - If you have children, you may have noticed that unless you buy a third-party application, it's difficult to manage and monitor what they are doing on the computer. The ability is now there to easily control what the children should have access to with quite a bit of granularity - allow or restrict specific games, specific website use, and even the times of day they can use it. Detailed reporting can also be used to follow-up on what they were doing.

- **Windows Mail** - If you have been an Outlook Express mail client user (different from the Microsoft Outlook mail client), then it might be important to know that Outlook Express has been renamed to Windows Mail and has been improved upon. It allows for instant search, better junk mail filtering to reduce spam, a phishing filter, and the data store size limit that the Outlook Express client had has been removed.

- **Windows Calendar** - This is new to the Windows operating system. A built in calendar allows you to manage your schedule. It has the ability to remind you of events, coordinate your schedule with others, and send or receive email appointments and invitations.

- **Media Capabilities** - The Windows Vista operating system includes some media features to help many of the day-to-day users that have gotten into digital photography, videography, etc.

    o Windows Photo Gallery allows you to easily work with photos - finding, organizing, editing, emailing, printing, and creating slide shows.

    o Windows Media Player 11 has been upgraded with a focus on better management and playback of digital media such as music and movies.

    o The new version of the Windows Movie Maker program allows you to easily import, organize, and edit digital home videos. It also allows you to easily create custom DVDs.

    o Windows Media Center, previously a separate product, is now built into Windows Vista. It brings together the ability to watch movies and TV, listen to music, and view pictures in one place using the Media Center menu or a remote control.

- **Improved Sharing** - Microsoft has tried to make sharing files and folders with other users on a network much simpler. A sharing wizard is now available to help you specify which users to you want to share information.

- **Diagnostics** - The Windows Vista OS includes the ability warn you of potential problems, such as a hard drive starting to go bad or an application that is taking up more and more memory. If the Windows Vista OS will not start up, a new "Startup Repair" technology will help take you through a step-by-step guide to get you back up and going while helping to prevent the least amount of data loss possible.

Overall, the Windows Vista operating system provides much better security and new and improved functionality. Do you as a user need this new operating system? Well, if you are buying a new computer then yes, you will want to make sure it comes with the Windows Vista operating system (see "The Basics of Buying a New Computer" section for more on the different versions). Having the latest operating system makes sense when buying a new computer - Microsoft will support it the longest, it will be more secure, it should provide a better user experience, and it will most likely be what is offered anyway from the manufacturer of the new computer.

Now, the next question is... should I upgrade my current version of Windows to the Windows Vista operating system? That's going to depend on many factors. If you're one of those people that always need the latest and the greatest, then you'll probably upgrade regardless of what I have to say.

If you're running an unsupported version of Windows (such as the Windows 95, Windows 98, Windows Me, or Windows NT® operating systems), then you should definitely make the move to the Windows Vista OS simply because those others are no longer supported. In addition, security is a MAJOR concern with these operating systems, and most new applications are not supported (and in some cases will not run) on the older versions of of the Windows OS. However, in your case, you will most likely need to buy a new computer in order to even meet the hardware requirements of Windows Vista.

If you're running the Windows 2000 OS, you might be a borderline candidate. Windows 2000 is arguably Microsoft's first solid operating system. However, as of this writing, it's going on seven years old. In technology years, that's a lifetime. Chances are, if you're running the Windows 2000 OS, you are probably getting to the point where you're considering getting a new computer. If that's the case, I would just stick with what you've got until you get the new computer.

If you're running the Windows XP OS, I wouldn't necessarily go running out the door to get the upgrade unless it provides something you really need. Just be sure that you have installed all critical updates (particularly a minimum of Service Pack 2) from the Microsoft Update site **(http://update.microsoft.com).** You may possibly already have the hardware required to run the Windows Vista operating system, but Windows XP is a very good operating system and it may not necessarily be worth the hassle of upgrading.

V. The Basics of Software

chapter 9

Software

What is it?

Software is usually referred to mean any program or application that runs on top of the operating system (such as Windows). Right now, I'm using the software Microsoft Word to create this book. There is so much software designed to run on the Windows operating system in this world it could make your head spin. There's software to manage your finances, create and edit websites, software to help make other software better, etc. In most cases, if there is something that you can think of that maybe a computer could help you with, someone has probably created a program that will do it.

Now, not all software is created equal. Programmers are the people who create software and some are better than others are at it. Some may write software that isn't as easy to use as a very similar piece of software that another programmer that writes. Some may not write the software that runs the same task as quickly as another does. Some don't add common sense features to a program... those are the times you are using software and think, "Now why won't it let me do what I want it to?"

The important thing to keep in mind is that you probably have a computer to make your life easier and maybe have some fun. The software you choose should be able to do most of what you want it to. How do you find that? Trial and error. Many software companies will let you download a "demo" version that will either run for a certain number of days or only let you do a limited number of functions until you purchase the full version. Also, look at what other people have to say about software that you are looking into to get a better idea of the quality of a product. Go to the Google™ search engine **(http://www.google.com)** or the Yahoo!® search engine **(http://www.yahoo.com)** and type in the name of the software you are interested in followed by the word "reviews." You will most likely find some interesting links to help you make a better decision.

When you first buy a computer, it usually comes with a bunch of software. That's a double-edged sword. On one hand, you have all kinds of software you can try out and see what you like. On the other hand, most computer manufacturers pre-install all the software on the computer. So, if you don't want it, you need to uninstall each of them individually.

What do I need?

The good news is that everyone's needs are different and there's likely a plethora of different applications that will provide most of what you need. The bad news is that means I can't really tell you what software you should or shouldn't get. I will however, give you some different options on some of the major categories to get you started and some of the pros and cons I have found with each of them.

Productivity suites

Productivity suites are packages that contain software that satisfy an essential part of most users' needs for a business. They usually include a word processing application and a spreadsheet application. However, they may also include other software such as a small database application, a slideshow presentation program, an email application, etc. Here are some examples...

Microsoft Office
The Microsoft Office software holds the largest market share for productivity suites and is generally considered to be the de facto standard. The current version, Office 2007, has eight different versions in itself available for purchase! To see the included software with the various editions, you'll want to head over to the Microsoft Office website - **http://office.microsoft.com**. Some of the more popular products available in Microsoft Office suite are:
- *Microsoft Word* - A word processing application
- *Microsoft Excel®* - A spreadsheet program
- *Microsoft PowerPoint®* - An application for creating slideshows
- *Microsoft Outlook®* - An email program and Personal Information Manager (PIM)
- *Microsoft Access™* - A database application
- *Microsoft Publisher* - A desktop publishing application

Because the Microsoft Office software holds such a large market share, competitors must strive to create office suites that are compatible with file types for this software. In other words, because a user may email another user a Microsoft Word document, the office suite the other user is using must be able to open that Word document. On the flip side, if a user creates a word processing document in something other than the Microsoft Office software, they generally want to be able to save it in a format that the Microsoft Word program can open to avoid compatibility problems.

Microsoft has now developed a new standard called Office Open XML formats in Office 2007 for the Word, Excel, and PowerPoint programs. What this means is that Microsoft has developed a standard for its documents that is open to all developers to use. This is a big deal because it means that other companies can more easily develop their own applications to open the new defaults for Office files as well as save files out to these formats. This will likely mean stronger competition for Microsoft in the long run, so it came as a surprise to many people in the technology industry when they decided to do this.

However, the Microsoft Office suite has been in use by so many people for so long, it is difficult for many companies to migrate to another application. It includes its own Visual Basic for Applications (VBA) that allows macros to be created to help expedite repetitive tasks. Many companies have hundreds of documents with macros already ingrained that would need to be rebuilt or converted to work with a different office suite - a huge undertaking for many companies.

Office 2007 Professional Edition has a retail price of about $499, while the Standard Edition retails for about $399. If you already own a previous version of the Microsoft Office suite, it will run you about $329 for the Professional Edition upgrade or about $239 for the Standard Edition upgrade. Details on these and other versions can be found at **http://office.microsoft.com**.

OpenOffice.org®

The OpenOffice.org suite is built on what is called open-source code. What that means is that anyone can obtain the actual programming code that makes the software work. The idea is that by sharing the code, programmers around the globe can see what makes the software tick and can help to make improvements to it to make it better. Many people confuse open-source software as being free. This is true in some cases, but the two are not synonymous. In the case of the OpenOffice.org software, however, the office suite is free to download and use. It can be obtained from the OpenOffice.org website - **http://www.openoffice.org.**

The included software includes:
  - Writer - A word processing application
  - Calc - A spreadsheet program
  - Impress - An application for creating slideshows
  - Base - A database application
  - Draw - A program to create documents using diagrams and graphics

What's made this software suite begin to gain momentum as a replacement to the Microsoft Office suite is that it operates very much like the Microsoft Office software and at a better price... *free!*

The current version of the OpenOffice.org suite as of this writing is 2.1.x. It provides a comparable interface to the Microsoft Office suite. There are differences, but for the most part, they operate very similarly. In addition, it provides the ability to open files created with the Microsoft Office software, such as Word or Excel files. It also provides the ability to save files you create with the OpenOffice.org suite in the Microsoft Office format. That way, if you send the file to someone who uses the Microsoft Office software, he or she can open the file.

The near $500 retail price of the Microsoft Office suite makes a lot of people cringe. Although in my opinion it's an excellent product, you can buy a new computer for that price. If you are very adept at using the Microsoft Office software, you may find the differences in the two products to be a little annoying. However, if you can save that much money to give a free software suite a chance, I'd say it's worth a shot. If you don't like it, you haven't wasted any money and you can still go out and purchase a suite such as Microsoft Office.

StarOffice®

The StarOffice software from Sun Microsystems® is marketed to be a low-cost alternative to the Microsoft Office software. It's built directly on the OpenOffice.org code and can run on either the Windows or Linux operating system. The current version as of this writing is Star Office™ 8.0. It includes the following:

- StarOffice 8 Writer - A word processing program
- StarOffice 8 Calc - A spreadsheet application
- StarOffice 8 Impress - A program for creating slideshows
- StarOffice 8 Base - A database application
- StarOffice 8 Draw - A program to create documents using diagrams and graphics

The StarOffice software suite has a list price for just shy of $70 - a much more reasonable price than the Microsoft Office suite in the minds of many people. So why not just download the OpenOffice.org software and skip the cost completely? For many users you can do just that and you'd be good to go, but for a lot of people, particularly businesses, the StarOffice software provides some additional things they can't live without, such as:

- A built-in spellchecker and a thesaurus
- Additional fonts, templates to use, sample documents, and clipart graphics
- StarOffice product support (certain stipulations apply)

More information on the StarOffice suite can be found at **http://www.sun.com/staroffice.**

There are plenty of other productivity suites that can be found... some good, some bad. You need to look around and find what works best for you. Some others include:

- **Corel® WordPerfect® Office - http://www.corel.com**
  o Around $300 for the standard version

- **Lotus® SmartSuite®** - http://www.lotus.com
  - o Around $250
- **Microsoft Works** - http://www.microsoft.com/products/works
  - o Around $100
- **GNOME Office** - http://www.gnome.org
  - o Free
- **602PC SUITE** - http://www.software602.com
  - o Around $40
- **EasyOffice™** - http://www.easyofficepremium.com
  - o Around $50
- **ThinkFree® Desktop** - http://www.thinkfree.com
  - o Around $50
  - o Online version is free for a basic account

Financial software

When I was getting close to finishing college around 1999, I had this idea in my head that I was financially stable. I had no idea where I stood with my money - school loans, credit card debts, etc. Nevertheless, I figured I was probably in good shape. Then, once I started working as a systems engineer, I ran across a product called Quicken®. I decided to mess around with it a little in the year 2000 and entered my financial information in it. It took a couple months before the software balanced everything out, but once it did, boy was I in for a shock. I owed more than I thought I did and didn't have any assets. But the Quicken software gave me a debt reduction plan that gave me a timeline of how much I needed to pay on each loan (credit cards, school loans, car loan, etc.) and also when I could get out of debt. I followed that thing religiously, and it took me until the end of 2005, but I finally got completely out of debt and would never have been able to do it without a product like Quicken. It's not that software got me out of debt - I did that - but without it, I never would have been able to get everything into perspective of exactly where I was at financially. Now half my life's in the Microsoft Outlook client and the other half is in the Quicken software.

As an added benefit, one of their major strengths lies in their ability to connect securely over the Internet to most major financial institutions and download your current activity. With a click of the button, I can see down to the penny exactly what my net worth is... that's very impressive to me.

There are two major competitors in the finance software arena - the Quicken software from Intuit and the Microsoft Money program. In the years that have gone by, they have both changed dramatically (for the better) and are both solid products. I tried changing over to the Microsoft Money software just to see if it had anything better to offer, but it was about the same and I already felt comfortable with how the Quicken program worked, so I still use that. Both products are extremely good, however.

- **Quicken** - http://www.quicken.com
  - o The current version as of this writing is Quicken 2007.
  - o The Quicken program offers different versions depending on your needs:
    - **Basic** - lists for around $30 and provides the basics for tracking bank accounts and credit cards.
    - **Deluxe** - lists for around $50 and provides everything in the Basic edition as well as tracking 401(k) and IRA plans, planning for college, retirement, or a new home, and helping find hidden tax deductions.
    - **Premier** - lists for around $70, provides everything in Deluxe, and allows you to monitor investment performance and minimize capital gains.
    - **Home & Business** - lists for around $80 and provides everything in the Premier version as well as the ability to manage certain aspects of small business finances.

- **Microsoft Money** - http://www.microsoft.com/money
  - o The current version as of this writing is Money 2007.
  - o Like the Quicken software, offers different versions depending on your needs:
    - **Essentials** - Lists for around $20 and provides the ability to track spending for your bank account.
    - **Deluxe** - Lists for around $50 and gives you everything in Essentials as well as managing credit and debit, planning for retirement, finding hidden tax deductions, and managing 401(k) accounts.
    - **Premium** - Lists for around $80 and gives you everything in Deluxe as well as helping to minimize capital gains and automate Schedule D tax reports.
    - **Home & Business** - Lists for around $90 and gives you everything Premium does plus functionality to manage certain aspects of small business finances.

Of course, this is only the tip of the iceberg. There are an infinite number of software applications out there to do just about anything you can dream of. As you become more familiar with the computer's capabilities, you will soon begin to realize how you can harness its strengths to help perform tasks that might otherwise be daunting to you. As that happens, use search engines and talk with other people to determine the software that may be exactly what you're looking for.

VI. The Basics of Email

chapter 10

Email

How it works

In order to work with your email, you either need to have some kind of email program that presents the information to you or you need to be able to access it through a web browser. Email works like this...

1. You compose an email in the email client and click send.
2. The email client then "talks" to "your" email server and gives it the information on the email - the message, who the email is addressed to, who you are, etc. Your email server is actually provided by whoever is hosting your email... like your Internet Service Provider (ISP) for instance in the case of most home users.
3. Your email server then looks at where the email is supposed to go, uses a telephone book type of lookup called DNS (short for Domain Name System) to determine who's responsible for taking care of mail for the recipient.
4. Your email server then "talks" to the email server of the addressee and passes along the same information it has - the message, who the email is addressed to, who you are, etc.
5. The recipient's email server then takes that email message and delivers it to the inbox of the addressee.
6. The addressee's email client regularly checks his/her email server for new messages. The next time it checks, it finds the email in the inbox and downloads it to the inbox of the email client for the recipient to read.

Kind of cool, huh?

In order to understand what kind of email client you need, you should understand a couple of technical terms... don't worry I'll try to keep it as painless as I can. Here are the most common ways that email clients get email from the mail server and present it to you.

POP3

The majority of home user accounts created by your ISP (the company that provides your connection to the Internet) allow you to get your email by using something called POP (Post Office Protocol). The current version is usually referred to as POP3. POP3 works by downloading messages from the inbox on the email server (usually your ISP) to the inbox of your email client. Generally, as the messages are downloaded to your email client's inbox, they are deleted from the mail server.

There are a couple concerns with POP3. One is that, as I said, messages are by default deleted from the server once they are downloaded. That means they now only exist on that one particular computer. You cannot view the messages from another computer because they can no longer be obtained from the server. This leads to another concern. Because all your email is stored on that one computer, if your computer hard drive was to crash, you would lose all your email if you do not perform backups of your hard drive. A third concern is that POP3 allows messages to be pulled only from the inbox of the email server. Any folders you create for organization must be created on the email client.

The largest concern, however, is that, although POP3 supports secure configurations, most of the time, the email client is configured in a way that when the email client contacts the server to check for new email for you, it sends your password across the Internet unencrypted. Essentially, what that means is if someone were to see the information passing from you to the email server (which does occur), they would be able to see your user name and password in plain text. With that information, they now have access to your account, plain and simple. Scary, isn't it?

IMAP

IMAP (short for Internet Message Access Protocol) is newer and is similar to POP3, but gives a little more flexibility. IMAP4 is the current version and is generally set up in a manner that the email is left on the email server until the user explicitly deletes the message(s). That means that unlike POP3, if you were to go to another computer and configure it to view your email, you would be able to see all of it. It also means in the event your hard drive crashes, your mail is still on the email server. In addition, by default, your password is never sent across the Internet in plain text for anyone lurking to be able to see. In addition, IMAP provides the ability to have multiple folders stored on the email server, rather than simply your inbox. The downsides... IMAP is more complex to create mail clients for and unfortunately, support for IMAP from email providers is usually not as common to see as it is for POP3.

Web Access

The majority of email providers now let you check your email using some type of web access using a web browser, such as Internet Explorer or Mozilla Firefox. How convenient is that?! You don't need to have an email client installed or configured - you simply open up the web browser, go to the web page, log in, and you're good to go. This provides the ability to quickly check your email from just about anywhere that has an Internet connection. Many companies have provided free accounts that have been letting you do this for years...Yahoo! Mail, Hotmail® (now Windows Live Mail), and the Google Mail™ (Gmail®) webmail services are among some of the largest. Additionally, the email is stored 100% on the email provider's mail server(s), meaning if your hard drive crashes, you don't lose any data. Additionally, that means you can see all your email anytime from any computer.

So what are the downsides? Up until recently, they were not always the quickest to work with. You would spend a lot of time clicking and then waiting for the action to take place. Now, however, this is quickly becoming a thing of the past. As new technologies such as AJAX (Asynchronous JavaScript® and XML) work their way into how websites are now developed, web access accounts are becoming as responsive as desktop email clients.

MAPI

This is a type of connection that is used in many corporate environments that use the Microsoft Outlook messaging and collaboration client with the Microsoft Exchange mail server program or that use the Novell® GroupWise® software. MAPI is not something that is generally used on home computers, but is worth noting because many people are familiar with interacting with this from their place of business. MAPI (Messaging Application Programming Interface) gives users the ability to manipulate all email locally and have the changes synchronized with the email server. It is quite effective in corporate environments.

General email clients

The following email clients are used to take advantage of an email address (or addresses) that are hosted by your Internet Service Provider (ISP). For example, when you sign up for DSL or cable Internet, the ISP may give you the option of creating email addresses based on their domain name, like **jimwhite@xyz-fake-dsl-company.com**. Many of these will let you use an email client listed below, a web access method of getting your email, or a combination of both.

These email clients are also used when you purchase your own domain name and then set up email under that domain name. A domain name is a publicly registered name. For example, Microsoft owns the domain name "microsoft.com" and they can then base their website off that domain name **(http://www.microsoft.com),** as well as their email addresses **[...]@microsoft.com**. We'll talk more about this later in the chapter.

Outlook Express/Windows Mail

Versions of the Windows operating system prior to the Windows Vista OS come with a built in email client called Outlook Express (not to be confused with Microsoft Outlook, the larger messaging and collaboration client that comes with some versions of the Microsoft Office) suite. With the Windows Vista operating system, Microsoft has revamped the Outlook Express client and renamed it to Windows Mail.

The Outlook Express and Windows Mail email clients allow you to work with POP3 and IMAP email accounts. The good news is that they are free (with Windows, of course) and will work with almost all email providers. A disadvantage to these email clients is that they are designed to be just that... email clients. If you are looking for something to be more of a Personal Information Manager (PIM), you'll want to look at something like the Microsoft Outlook messaging client.

Thunderbird®

The Thunderbird email client is offered as an alternative to the Outlook Express and Windows Mail clients. It is developed by Mozilla® and is currently available for download from **http://www.mozilla.com/thunderbird**. It is a free application and offers much of the same functionality as its competitor. Personally, I think the Windows Mail email client appears to offer built-in capabilities that will suit the majority of home users just fine. However, there are some differences between the two products and if the Windows Mail client does not provide you with what you are after, it may be worth trying out the Thunderbird software.

Microsoft Outlook

I love Microsoft Outlook. As scary as it is, I have built my life around it and it only seems to get better with each new version. The Microsoft Outlook messaging client is a full-blown Personal Information Manager (PIM). What this means is that it offers the ability to organize and manage many types of personal information. In essence, it acts as an electronic personal organizer. It provides the ability to do calendaring (with reminders) for appointments, birthdays, anniversaries, etc. For instance, I have my family and close friends' birthdays all in my calendar with a reminder that pops up on the screen usually a couple days before their birthday letting me know that it's coming up. I have a horrible memory, so this works wonders for me! It also has sections for address books, tasks that need to be done (again with reminders if desired), and a handy feature for notes which help take the place of all those scrap pieces of paper you have laying around everywhere. Oh, yeah... and it manages email (POP3, IMAP, MAPI, etc.).

The downside is that this one isn't included with the Windows operating system and is not free. It is either available as a standalone product or bundled in with certain editions of the Microsoft Office suite. If you are going to be purchasing the Microsoft Office software and are interested in a Personal Information Manager such as the Outlook client, it makes sense to go with the edition that includes it. However, if you are using or planning to use an alternative office productivity suite, you may not have a mail client (other than the built-in Outlook Express or Windows Mail software). In that case, if you want something more powerful, buying the Microsoft Outlook client as a standalone product makes sense. The current version of the Microsoft Outlook software is Outlook 2007 and as a standalone program has a list price of about $110. More information on the Microsoft Outlook client can be found at **http://www.microsoft.com/outlook**.

There are so many email clients available - some free and some not. If the above-mentioned clients do not do what you would like them to, here are some other alternatives:

- **Eudora® - http://www.eudora.com**
  - o Offers three different options ranging from free to around $20 per year
- **Pegasus Mail® - http://www.pmail.com**
  - o Free - one of the original email clients
- **IncrediMail® - http://www.incredimail.com**
  - o Free - with the goal of making email "fun," offers animations, backgrounds, emoticons, and more

Free email accounts

There is an issue with using an email address provided by your Internet Service Provider (ISP). Let's say that you're using DSL from the XYZ DSL Company and they offer you the ability to create your own email addresses based off their domain name they own (xyz-dslcompany.com). You create an email address of **jimwhite@xyz-fake-dsl-company.com**, you're sending and receiving mail, and life is good. Then a year later, they raise their prices big time, you're not happy with their service, or you move to an area where XYZ DSL Company does not provide service. That's where the fun begins. You now have to do the following:

- Get a new email address somewhere.
- Let your family and friends know that your email address changed.
- Log in to any websites you have accounts with and change your contact email address (which in some cases is your user name).
- Possibly move all your old email to your new account.

What a long and painful process! No one wants to do that! So how do you avoid all that? You need to take that into consideration from the beginning.

You can get your own domain name that you own, which means that you also own any email addresses you want based off that domain name. And again, I'll detail this some more later in this chapter.

But what if you don't want to pay for your own domain name? If you just want an email address that you can hang onto for a long time, one that's not dependent on you moving, changing ISP's, etc., why not use a web access account from one of the big guys available to you free of charge? They have become very easy to use, can be accessed from anywhere with an Internet connection, and you don't need to install or configure any email software on your computer. And as I mentioned earlier, newer technologies have enabled the development of email web clients to be as responsive and advanced as full clients such as Outlook Express or Windows Mail. Here's a few of the more recognized ones...

Yahoo! Mail

The Yahoo! Mail webmail service is probably the most well known of all the free email accounts out there. You simply go to **http://mail.yahoo.com** and signup for an account. As of this writing, they offer 1 Gigabyte of storage for your email, which should be plenty for the typical user. If it's not, they offer upgraded pay plans to give you more storage as well as some other options. Your email account also gives you an address book, a calendar, and a notepad. In addition, your account will then tie into a ton of services that you can access - games, maps, shopping, etc. I have an email account through Yahoo! that I use constantly for all my personal needs and have had the account for over ten years.

Hotmail/Windows Live Mail

The Hotmail webmail service has been around since the mid 90's. It is being replaced by its new version called Windows Live Mail. It is similar to Yahoo! in that the account gives you an address book and calendar and ties you into all kinds of other services that you can then access. To get a Windows Live Mail webmail account, go to **http://mail.live.com**. I have a Hotmail/Windows Live Mail account that I obtained around the time the Hotmail service became available. This used to be my primary email account, but now I use it mostly as my email address for when I order things online.

Gmail

Google is newer to the web based mail game, but has gained popularity very quickly, due in part to how happy people have become with the Google search engine. Gmail webmail service is using storage as their claim to fame. Much of the marketing for the Gmail service is that you shouldn't have to ever delete your email (spam being the exception). They continue to add storage to the servers that store your email and then continue to pass that storage onto you. A Gmail webmail account currently offers about 2.75 Gigabytes of storage and continues to grow. I have a Gmail account that I use for testing and for quick storage.

As you may have noticed, I have several email accounts that I use. Some I use just for spam - such as a website that requires a legitimate email address, but I know they are going to send me garbage as soon as I give them my address. So, I keep a couple accounts separate just for this. They're free and I can easily dispose of one and get another if one starts to receive too much spam. I use a fantastic free utility called ePrompter® (**http://www.eprompter.com**), which monitors all my accounts at the same time for new email. When I need to dig in closer to a particular email, then I'll go to the actual mail site.

Personalized email accounts

So, you've decided that you want your own email address - something not branching off some other company's domain. Why have an email address of **jimwhite@xyz-fake-dsl-company.com** or be based off one of the free web-access email services and have an address of something along the lines of **jimwhite@free-email-addresses-123.com**? Why not do something that's more professional and is yours? Why not be have something like **jimwhite@booksbyjim.com**?

It's not as difficult as you would think. In order to do this, you must first purchase **booksbyjim.com** or whatever domain you can think of. Here's the catch - someone can't already own it. There can only be one **booksbyjim.com** on the Internet. To check, you can go to any of the reputable big guys on the Internet that allow you to purchase domain names. Here's just a few of them...

- **Network Solutions® - http://www.networksolutions.com**
- **GoDaddy® - http://www.godaddy.com**
- **Register.com® - http://www.register.com**

Once you go to one of these sites, they all have a section to immediately search for a domain name to see if anyone owns it. In our case, we'll type in "booksby_jim" (without the quotes) and select ".com." After doing a quick search, it should then tell you if the domain name is available or if someone else owns it. If no one else owns it, you can then purchase the domain name.

You now have some options. If you would like Network Solutions or whoever to take care of everything for you (email, website if you want one, etc.), you can do that and it should all be fairly straightforward. Currently, on Network Solutions, for the whole kit and caboodle, it will probably run you about $10 per month.

NOTE: If you have your own email server or web server or would like someone else to take care of that piece for you, you can just purchase the domain name by itself. This however is going to require a little more technical expertise to get set up.

Now that you've bought your domain name with email services, you should be able to set up the email account you want. You can create a "jim white" account, or whatever you desire. The full email address will be the account followed by the "@" sign and whatever your domain name is.

There should be instructions available from Network Solutions or any provider you have used as to how to configure your email client so you can get and send mail now as **jimwhite@booksbyjim.com**." As an added bonus, you may have gotten free website hosting from the company, so if you want to, you can set up your own webpage... **www.booksbyjim.com**.

Now that's some good stuff!

VII. The Basics of Protecting Your Computer

chapter 11

Viruses, Spyware, Etc.

Unfortunately, with every good thing, there are bad things that come with it. Such is the case with the Internet and email. Email has made communication quick, easy, and convenient. The Internet has streamlined how research is done and helped small businesses easily become global competitors. Nevertheless, both email and the Internet have also become a stomping ground for the bad guys. I can tell you that if you're thinking that nothing will happen to your computer if you don't protect it, you'll most likely be learning a lesson the hard way.

That being said, let's go over some of the current Internet and email concerns and how you can protect yourself.

Viruses and such

Most people try to lump the different malicious programs into the category of viruses. However, that's not really the case. There are four types of these generally malicious programs, each a little different:

- **Viruses** - A virus attaches itself to a file in order to spread itself and infect other computers. Viruses cannot run without interaction, meaning a user must first launch the program in order for it to do anything. This is why you have probably heard people warn you not to open any attachments, even from someone you know, if you are unsure about the attachment.
- **Worms** - Worms are similar to viruses, but have the ability to spread themselves without interaction. These have the capability to spread themselves to everyone in your address book, for example.
- **Trojan Horses** - Trojan horses disguise themselves. For example, you think you have installed one application, but what you don't know is that the program installs a second program as well, a Trojan horse. Some Trojan horses are not as malicious as others are, but some create a back door, or a way for someone to gain access to your computer.
- **Rootkits** - Rootkits are newer to the scene and can be close to impossible to remove. They often make themselves a part of the operating system and are able to hide even from many anti-virus or anti-spyware utilities.

Now let's talk about what generally happens. Usually a virus has an objective to do some type of damage - whether to take up all the memory in your computer and slow it to a crawl or to delete all the files on your computer. Regardless of the payload, I've never met a virus that I liked.

So why on earth would anyone develop a program to do this? Of course there are your malicious people that write these pieces of code to cause damage or to gain access to users' computers. Sometimes people have a grudge against another company and write code that will be spread to other computers and use those computers (called "zombies") to attack the targeted company's website. Sometimes people do it just to see if they can... these may even be kids learning how to program and, in some cases, not realizing what the code is capable of doing.

It is absolutely critical that you have software on your computer to protect you from viruses. It is also critical that the software is always kept up to date. Software made to protect your computer against viruses is called anti-virus software.

Almost all paid anti-virus software is subscription-based. This means you pay a subscription fee on a regular basis, generally a year, in order to get updates to protect you against the latest viruses.

Many new computers come with anti-virus software already preinstalled on the computer. The problem is that most people let it go at that. Eventually the subscription expires and now the computer is unprotected against any virus that comes out after the date the subscription expired.

Having anti-virus software without keeping it up to date is almost as bad as not running any anti-virus software at all. It will almost surely lead to you getting a virus at some point.

Before we continue, I would like to clear up something that occurs quite often that many people find confusing. As I mentioned, sometimes a worm will spread itself to everyone in an infected users address book. Here's where it can get confusing. Let's say Joe's computer is infected with a worm. The worm then goes through his address book and sends itself out via email to everyone it finds. The twist is that this particular worm changes the "From" address. This particular worm picks a name in the address book (let's say Lisa) and makes the email appear that it's coming from Lisa. Now, let's say that Dawn was one of the people in Joe's address book that received this email with the worm attached. Dawn was running up to date anti-virus software, which caught the email, eliminated the worm from her computer, and alerted Dawn to it. Dawn looks at the message and sees that it came from Lisa (or so she thinks). Dawn calls Lisa and says, "Hey you just sent me a virus!" Lisa is confused. She's running up to date anti-virus software. Just in case though, she scans her computer and of course, it comes up clean.

See how this can be confusing? In addition, no one knows it was from Joe, who probably will continue to send out the virus without even knowing it. Nothing can really be done until Joe decides to update his anti-virus, or replaces or reinstalls his computer. ***Thanks a lot Joe!***

I'll discuss some of the ways to help prevent viruses in "Chapter 14 - Security Management."

Spyware/Adware

In general, most users now understand how to deal with viruses. We know not to open up emails (especially attachments) from people we don't know. We know not to run programs we are unsure of.

The current problem we are now working to get better control of is spyware. There are two categories that usually are labeled as spyware:

- **Spyware** - Spyware is software that is installed on a user's computer without the user's consent. It is similar to Trojan horses in that many times it will piggyback itself with software that you download and install. The difference between spyware and viruses is that spyware generally does not spread itself to other computers. Spyware does things as simple as constantly changing your web browser homepage all the way to tracking user information and reporting it back to a third party.
- **Adware** - Adware generally is installed with certain applications, sometimes with the user knowing and sometimes not. It then displays ads, usually as pop-ups, sometimes all over the screen.

Spyware is horrible. In many cases, it is worse than viruses. It can render a computer useless. There have been many times I have seen a computer beat up so bad with spyware there was no alternative but to format the computer and reinstall everything - not a fun thing to do and extremely time consuming.

Many anti-virus software vendors have taken it upon themselves to be the protectors of spyware and adware in addition to viruses. When choosing anti-virus software, you will find that, in most cases, it includes anti-spyware capabilities as well. The Windows Vista operating system comes with a built-in anti-spyware program called Windows Defender that, although not perfect, provides at least some level of protection.

In "Chapter 14 - Security Management," I'll talk about some ways to help prevent spyware and adware.

chapter 12

Spam and Phishing

<u>Spam</u>

Other than SPAM® being the infamous spiced ham in a can from Hormel®, spam has taken on its own meaning in the technology realm. Spam is electronic junk mail. Everyone that has an email address has probably gotten spam at one time or another... if you haven't then you're definitely the exception to the rule.

Emails with subjects like "V-I-A-G-A-R-A" or "Get a free TV!!" or "Find your perfect match"... why on earth do people send out millions of spam messages to people all over the globe? Do they think that people are actually going to respond?

Believe it or not, the answer is "Yes." People DO respond. Probably only a very small percentage, but think about it - if only two people out of 250 people were to click through on a piece of junk email, that's not very impressive. But, let's say a spammer sends that email out to 2,000,000 people. Now the number of people that respond has gone up to about 16,000! And, unlike all the junk mail you get at home from the postal service, the spammer doesn't have the cost of postage to pay for. There are also not limits to the number of messages a mail server can process. As long as the server has enough "oomph," it is possible to send out an unbelievable amount of email. So, now you can see that this has some potential to be lucrative.

But I don't want spam and I'm guessing you don't want spam. So, how do we combat it? Well, this has definitely been an uphill battle, but fortunately, the defenses have gotten much better over the years.

The problem all lies in two areas... false positives and false negatives. How do you determine that a piece email is actually junk mail? Imagine that you and your friend Bridgette are at work talking about how unbelievably high your car insurance rates are (I know - a boring conversation). She is in disbelief when you tell her how much you are paying and she says..."I can't remember the person's name I talked to at my insurance company, but he helped me bring my rates down tremendously. Once I find his name, I'll email you the information." Sounds like a good deal.

The next day she sends you an email with a subject of "Better car insurance rates." In the email, she repeats a couple things that you had talked about regarding how you should look into this other insurance company to lower your rates.

Now compare this to a piece of junk mail with the title "Better car insurance rates" that discusses how you should look into this other insurance company to lower your rates.

You and I can both tell which is the unsolicited junk email, but how can a software application do the same thing? That's the type of problem that developers run into. False positives occur when the spam filter sees a piece of legitimate email as being spam when in fact it's not. False negatives occur when anti-spam software thinks a piece of junk mail is legitimate, but is actually spam.

Fortunately, they have gotten better at it. Don't ask me how it works internally, but I can tell you that some programs are better at figuring out what's junk mail and what's not. Some anti-spam software has the ability to "learn" the difference between good and bad email based on what you've decided is legitimate and what is spam.

There are many different types of anti-spam software (and hardware) that are on the market today and there is no product that will be able to be 100% correct in identifying legitimate email versus junk email. In larger environments with hundreds or thousands of users, it is not uncommon to find that when email comes in, it actually passes through multiple spam filters to help ensure that almost all junk mail is caught.

In the case of most home and small business users, however, this is not usually a cost effective solution. Many times the email provider will provide junk mail filtering - this includes free web access email providers like Yahoo! Mail or the Gmail webmail service, as well as most email services that the Internet Service Provider (ISP) of your cable or DSL connection to the Internet provides.

On another level, there are also software applications that can run on a computer that will help filter this email for non-web based email clients. Here are a couple examples:

- **McAfee® SpamKiller®** - This software helps prevents spam from reaching your inbox and helps you identify email scams. It runs about $35 for a one-year subscription.
  http://www.mcafee.com
- **CA™ eTrust™ Anti-Spam** - This software will help filter out the email you don't want and deliver you the email you do want. All other email is sent to a quarantine area, which allows you to review it later. It runs about $30 for a one-year subscription.
  http://www.ca.com

If you are using an email client such as current versions of Microsoft Outlook or Windows Mail, they have anti-spam software built-in that will provide an extra layer of protection.

Phishing

Phishing is a term given to the technique that is used to try to lure end users into giving away sensitive information such as credit card information or user names and passwords. Generally, they appear as emails or instant messages.

An example might be an email that you receive that says that your bank is upgrading its software and needs you to confirm your account information. When you look at the email, it looks official. It has the bank's logo on it, makes sense, and has a link in the email that shows the bank's website address. You click on the link and it takes you to the bank's website... or so you think. It looks exactly like the website you've gone to before to check on your account balance. In the web browser's address bar, it has the bank's address in it, so it must be legit, you think.

What you don't know is that the link you clicked on took you to a website designed to look exactly like the bank's website. So, how did it get the bank's website address (also known as a URL or Uniform Resource Locator) in the address bar? In this example, when the bogus website loaded, it ran a script that put a picture of a fake address bar with the bank's real URL address covering the bogus address bar.

Then it prompts you to enter in your account details to ensure that your account is transferred over successfully during the "software upgrade." Before you know it, you've just willingly handed over your bank account information to a perfect stranger. **How's that for frightening?!**

This is just one example of the many phishing scams that come out on a regular basis. Many phishing emails look and claim to be from eBay®, PayPal®, or your bank, all trying to gain access to your account information. What kind of software do you need to make sure that you aren't suckered into one of these phishing scams?

Well, before we talk about some of the available software, the easiest way to avoid being scammed is to be suspicious of emails and instant messages like the above example. It is **extremely** rare for any legitimate company to ever ask for your account information, especially by email. In fact, I do not know of any company that will ever ask for your information. If you see an email that makes you wonder, it is most likely not legitimate. Call up the company and find out... chances are they'll tell you to delete the email immediately because it's a fraud.

Another sometimes helpful tactic is to go directly to the website of the company. If the email seems legitimate and has a link that you *know* is legitimate, instead of clicking on the link in the email, open up your web browser (Internet Explorer for instance) and type in the web address yourself and see what comes up. You might be wondering why.

Well, web links (called hyperlinks) do not always act as they appear. Let's say you go to a company's website and see a hyperlink that says "Human Resources." You click on it and it takes you to a different place on the company's website that gives you useful information regarding the human resources department... useful for websites when used in the right way. Well, the "bad guys" have figured out a way to use this to their advantage. Since the text can be anything and the hyperlink can take you to a page on the same website or to a completely different website, they make links appear to be something they are not. An example might be seeing a hyperlink that says "**http://www.XYZ-I-Am-Your-Bank.com.**" Well, just because the text says that, doesn't mean that's where it's taking you. In this example, the link actually takes you to "**http://ReadyToRipYouOff.com**" which is ready to do just that.

Sometimes though, it's comforting to have software installed that helps make sure you don't do the wrong thing. Many of the security suites have this functionality already built in. I'll talk about those in "Chapter 14 - Security Management."

As a side note, the Internet Explorer 7 web browser, has been released for the Windows XP OS (and is already built into the Windows Vista OS). The Internet Explorer 7 browser has the ability to provide some anti-phishing capabilities.

chapter 13

Firewalls

Many hackers try to find a "soft spot" to be able to get into your computer from somewhere else on the Internet. As Internet connectivity has become quicker than the old dial-up connections, hackers have been able to develop more sophisticated tools to be able to find the weak points of a computer. Because of this, it has become critical that your computer is protected from the bad guys on the outside.

Many DSL routers or cable modems can help aid in the process of protecting you by using something called Port Address Translation, also known as PAT. In a simplified scenario, your Internet Service Provider gives you a unique address that can be used on the Internet known as a public IP address. The router will give you (and any other computers connected on the inside) a different address known as a private IP address. The router then takes care of letting all users on the inside share the public IP address. Because PAT in essence "hides" your address from the Internet, it becomes a major layer of protection. Traffic on the Internet will not be able to easily get to your computer without specifically being allowed through on the DSL router or cable modem.

You can find out if you have a private IP address (and are therefore using PAT) by doing the following:

- Click on the "Start" button and in the search box, type in **cmd**, and then press the "ENTER" key.

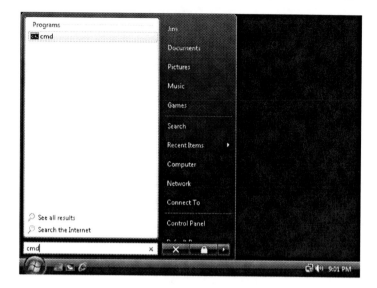

A black command-line box should then appear. Type in **ipconfig** and then hit the "Enter" key. You may see more than one type of connection defined, but generally, the one you'll be looking for will have address information already populated.

In the Windows Vista operating system, support for a different, up-and-coming IP standard is already built in (IP version 6), so it gets a little more complex than what many people were used to in previous versions of the Windows OS. However, IPv6 is not used very much yet, so you'll most likely want to look for the IP version 4, which is found in the line that says "IPv4 Address." Your IP address is the string of numbers to the right of that. In my case, as seen below, my IP address is "192.168.1.102."

You'll know if you have a private address because it will be in one of the following formats:
- 10.x.x.x
- 172.16.x.x through 172.31.x.x
- 192.168.x.x

If it begins with anything else, your router is not doing PAT (at least not correctly). Although PAT will drastically help protect you from hackers on the outside, a firewall should always be considered the most critical protection.

You can click on the "X" in the top right when you are ready to close the command prompt box.

A firewall is designed to perform one main job: control what is permitted and is not permitted to go from one network to another. In our case, one network is our home or home office. The other network is the Internet.

There are two types of firewalls - hardware and software. A hardware firewall is a device that is set up between your Internet router and all computers on your inside network. It is generally used by places with more than a few users or computers due to it being able to be centrally managed as well as the potentially higher cost. An administrator can determine what traffic can leave or get to the internal network.

A software firewall is sometimes referred to as a personal firewall. A software firewall runs on a computer such as your home computer and still keeps true to the firewall's purpose - keeping control of traffic. Once a software firewall is installed, it watches everything that takes place on the computer. The way it works with most personal firewalls is that if anything tries to get into your computer from the outside, the firewall will prevent it by default.

In most software firewalls, you must specifically tell it if you want the computer to be accessed from another computer anywhere else. For instance, in the Windows XP Professional and Windows Vista operating systems, there is a built-in ability to remotely control your computer from anywhere in the world (using Remote Desktop). However, the first time you tried to access your computer from another computer, most configurable firewalls will then display a pop-up box asking you if it's alright for that particular computer to have access to your computer using that particular type of interface (called a port). In this case, the port would be TCP 3389, known as the Remote Desktop Protocol (RDP). Once you've received that pop-up box and tell it something like "Yes, I'd like to always allow access for this type of connection from the outside," then the next time you try to connect, the personal firewall should let the connection happen.

It's critical to understand the importance of what you are doing when you allow access through a port from anywhere however. Every port that is allowed access from the outside then becomes a security risk. Now any hacker from the outside that does a port scan and finds that port open on your IP address can then connect to your computer using that port. In the example above, the hacker would see that the port is TCP 3389 and would then know that the open port is for Remote Desktop connections. He/she could then connect to your IP address and port number and would receive the same prompt for a user name and password that you see. In most cases, they would assume that a user name of "Administrator" exists on the computer and would now only need to figure out the password. And, a hacker usually doesn't do this manually. The hacker likely will use an automated tool to go through hundreds of passwords per second until the right one is found. What I'm saying is this - if you don't have a dire need to allow access to your computer from outside your home or home office, don't do it.

The Windows XP OS comes with a firewall, but it only monitors incoming traffic. So, if you used that firewall and got a virus that somehow was able to get past your anti-virus software, the virus could potentially send itself out to anyone in your address book without you knowing. This was corrected with the Windows Vista operating system, which has a Windows Firewall that monitors both incoming and outgoing connections. However, outgoing connections are allowed by default and unfortunately changing the default to "block" makes exceptions not very easy to configure. Both the Windows XP and Windows Vista operating system firewalls are better than nothing, but if you are not using a security suite with a firewall (to be discussed in "Chapter 14 - Security Management"), I would recommend using a third-party firewall. Moreover, many are free! Here are a couple examples:

- **Sunbelt Kerio Personal Firewall®** - This firewall was created by Kerio™ and recently bought by Sunbelt Software®. There are two versions of the firewall - a free and full version The full version runs about $20 a year and provides extras such as content filtering. For the typical user though, the free version does provide the basics of network monitoring and is very configurable.
  http://www.sunbelt-software.com
- **ZoneAlarm®** - ZoneAlarm is a personal firewall from Zone Labs® that is considered by many to be very user friendly and therefore has gained quite a following.
  http://www.zonelabs.com

chapter 14

Security Management

All-in-one products

By now you're probably thinking, "How the heck am I supposed to manage all of this? I thought computers were supposed to make life easier, not more difficult!" Well, the good news is that many vendors have created products that will do all or most of the things we talked about. In my case, computers are what I know best - so I like to try out different types of software to get familiar with the good and bad. Nevertheless, it does take time and in almost all cases, I can imagine that you don't want to waste your time trying to manage all the individual types of software. Therefore, I would strongly suggest getting an all-in-one application to take care of all of this for you. Generally, it will be less of a hassle to manage and will integrate better than if you had separate components by different companies. Here are the key components that should be integrated into the suite:

- **Anti-virus**
- **Anti-spam**
- **Personal firewall**
- **Anti-spam/Anti-phishing**
- **Parental controls**
- **Privacy controls**

Here are a few of my suggestions for an all-in-one security suite:

- **ZoneAlarm Internet Security Suite** - Zone Labs is best known for their personal firewall. They have their own security suite. It runs about $70 per year and can be considered one of the cheapest prices you'll ever pay for security. This would probably be the one product that I suggest you ensure is used on each computer you have in your home or home office.
  http://www.zonelabs.com
- **Norton Internet Security™** - This suite is probably one of, if not the most, popular suites available. This is another very good product that I would recommend if you're looking for an alternative to the "ZoneAlarm Internet Security Suite." It also runs about $70 per year.
  http://www.symantec.com
- **McAfee® Internet Security Suite** - This product is similar to the "Norton Internet Security™" suite in what it provides for security. Staying in line with the others, it also runs about $70 per year. I haven't actually worked much with this product, but McAfee is a solid anti-virus vendor and another leader in the market.
  http://www.mcafee.com
- **eTrust™ Internet Security Suite** - Made by another well-known security company, CA™. Again, around $70 per year.
  http://www.ca.com
- **Trend Micro® Internet Security (PC-cillin®)** - Trend Micro makes anti-virus that I highly recommend on most servers. In the home and home office, they have now become a major player on the desktop as well. The difference in their suite is that it only runs around $50 per year.
  http://www.trendmicro.com
- **Microsoft Live OneCare™** - Microsoft is new to the anti-virus game, but they are doing their best to make it as easy to use as possible for users, which has helped them gain some market share. It runs about $50 per year.
  http://www.windowsonecare.com

My laptop security

In case you're wondering which software I use, here is what I am currently running on my laptop... but also remember, I try out different software in order to be sure that I am familiar with it:

- **Anti-Virus**
  - *AVG® Anti-Virus from Grisoft®* - **http://www.grisoft.com**
  - I change out this software somewhat frequently to test out other anti-virus software.
  - I also run periodic scans using other vendor's free plugins from their websites such as:
    - Trend Micro HouseCall® - **http://housecall.trendmicro.com**

- **Anti-Spyware**
  - o *Microsoft Windows Defender -* **http://www.microsoft.com/athome/security/spyware/software/default.mspx**
  - o I also run periodic scans using other vendor's free tools such as:
    - Trend Micro HouseCall - **http://housecall.trendmicro.com**
    - Spybot® Search & Destroy - **http://www.safer-networking.org**
- **Anti-Spam**
  - o *Yahoo! Mail's Built in Spam Protection -* My main personal account is from Yahoo! and gets very little junk mail. One of the biggest reasons I get very little junk mail is that I never use this account for anything except for communication with my family and friends. I have a number of other free web-mail accounts that I use as "disposable" addresses for signing up on other websites, ordering products from websites, etc. If one of the accounts starts getting an abundance of junk mail, I ditch it and sign up for another... no muss, no fuss. **http://mail.yahoo.com**
- **Anti-Phishing**
  - o *Yahoo! Mail's -* As I just mentioned, I only use my main account from Yahoo! for communication with my family and friends. Because of that, if that account gets an email from something, such as eBay or PayPal, I usually just mark it as spam. If, however, it does seem like an email that could be something legitimate, like my bank, I will not click on any link within the message. I will always go directly to the company's website and try to get to what I need to from there. If I have any questions, I simply call the company to verify. **http://mail.yahoo.com**
- **Firewall**
  - o When I was running Windows XP, I was using the Sygate® Personal Firewall, which was free. Sygate discontinued its free firewall in November 2005. However, this was my favorite of all the software firewalls. It is simple to configure and it works. Now that I am running Windows Vista, I am using the Windows integrated firewall. However, I will be working more with the Sunbelt Kerio Personal Firewall and ZoneAlarm firewall very soon.

Automatic updates

Let me start on the subject of updates by saying if you don't keep your software up to date, you are probably opening yourself up to some major security risks. There are always new vulnerabilities being discovered in software products that can put your computer at risk, and in some cases, allow a hacker to be able to take over your computer. These can be vulnerabilities in the Windows operating system, your word processing software, or even the anti-virus software itself. The good news is that the software vendors are generally very quick to "fix" the problems with their software and make available what's known as a "patch" to fix the problem. The bad news is that you need to be sure that you are keeping your software up to date.

Fortunately, more and more software makers are developing their software to auto-update itself - meaning occasionally it will connect to the vendor's website to check for updates. If it finds an update, it will either automatically install the update or it will let you know it found an update and prompt you to install it.

Some people may tell you not to let software automatically update itself. They may tell you it's in your best interest to manually check for and install one update (or patch) for a piece of software and then restart your computer to make sure everything runs without problems. The reason for this is that if for some reason the update causes problems on your computer and more than one update was installed on your computer, it will make it more difficult to troubleshoot what caused the problem - was it the update for the Windows operating system or the patch for the Adobe® Acrobat® Reader® or Microsoft Word software?

Here's what I'll tell you... If you have the time to check each piece of software for updates and test each of them, then I would highly recommend doing it because it definitely gives you more control. However, I know that time is a valuable commodity, so I will tell you that if you don't have the time or simply don't want to worry about it, then let the software update itself. Yes, there can come a time when a conflict can occur, but for as long as I've been doing this, I've been seeing less and less of these. In addition, if you're using the Windows XP or Windows Vista operating systems, a technology called System Restore is turned on by default. System Restore automatically takes periodic snapshots of your computer and allows you to do just what it says - restore your system back to the way it was before the problem occurred. And, the System Restore technology is even more efficient in the Windows Vista OS. It's not full proof, but does give you some added protection in the case that a major problem would occur.

The main thing you want to make sure stays updated are Microsoft products. Microsoft has made it easy to ensure that the Windows OS, the Microsoft Office software, the Windows Defender program, etc. stay updated. The first thing you should do is head over to Microsoft Update.

In the Windows Vista OS, you no longer use the Internet Explorer browser to use Microsoft Update, as you did in the Windows XP OS. To get to Microsoft Update, you can click on the "Start" button, select "Control Panel," and then choose "Check for updates" under the "Security" section. Then select the "Check for updates" link in the left pane.

I would strongly recommend installing ALL updates, including any Windows Service Packs, unless you know of an incompatibility with a software application that you are running. Microsoft deems most patches as important - updates and security fixes to problems that would otherwise leave your computer vulnerable or having the potential to cause performance problems.

All the updates that were selected will then be installed and once they are done, if any updates required a restart, you will be prompted to do so. If prompted, it is highly recommended to restart immediately after installing the updates.

Once you've restarted (if required), go back to the Microsoft Update site, and again do another "Check for updates." Sometimes there is an update that requires another update to be installed first. If that happens, you may see additional updates listed again. You will definitely want to install these as well and again, restart if necessary. This should be done until no updates are listed.

Some of the updates are for other parts of the Windows Vista operating system that I would also recommend installing. These updates are not usually rated as "Important," but can improve how some programs, features, or devices work. These are usually listed as "Recommended" or "Optional."

An example might be software for your printer. Major vendors work with Microsoft to ensure that their software can stay current as well. Therefore, if you have an HP® or Dell® printer for example, and an update is found for the software that controls your printer, you can install it right from here. This is an area where some people may tell you "if it ain't broke... don't fix it." However, when a manufacturer such as HP or Dell releases an update, it generally includes fixes for problems they are aware of and may fix compatibility issues with other products. I am an advocate of running up to date software with everything. In this case, I always install everything from the Microsoft Update site. Now I will leave that in your hands to decide what side of the fence you fall on. Remember, you can also just pick and choose what to install from here. Maybe you've been having a quirky printing issue that's been driving you nuts. In that case, it will probably be a good idea to install any update for your printer that it shows. It should bring you to the current version and may fix your problem.

The next question you might be thinking is... "How often do I need to update this stuff? I have better things to do!" To answer that, I have some good news. When you get a new computer, you will definitely want to make sure that everything is up to date from the Microsoft Update as a priority. Other than that,

Microsoft currently releases updates once a month (currently on the second Tuesday of the month) unless a highly critical update needs to be released. You can configure the "Automatic Updates" feature in Windows to do the job of keeping your computer up to date for you. Here's how to do this in Windows Vista OS...

- Click on the "Start" button and in the search box, type in **wuapp.exe**, and then press the "ENTER" key.

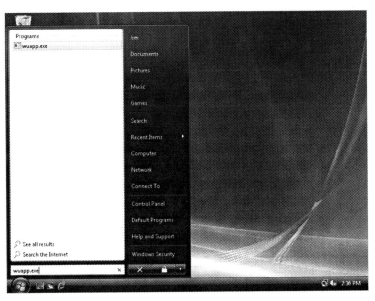

- When the "Windows Update" screen appears, click the link in the left for "Change settings."

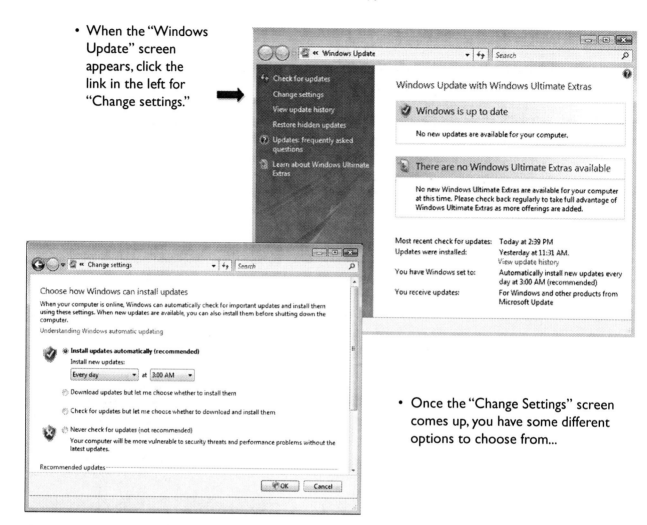

- Once the "Change Settings" screen comes up, you have some different options to choose from...

o **Install updates automatically (recommended)** - Microsoft recommends that you select this box to allow you to have your computer check for updates on a daily basis at a specified time when it's likely you're not working on the computer (such as 3:00 AM - the default). If any updates are found, it will install them without any interaction. When it's done installing the updates, if a restart is required, it will automatically restart the computer. If you leave your computer on all the time and don't leave anything open that you're working on, this may be a good option for you. The problem I have with this is that if you left anything open, such as a Microsoft Word document that you were working on and forgot to save changes on recently (shame, shame!), it is possible to lose those changes.

o **Download updates but let me choose whether to install them** - This is the option I choose on my laptop. Periodically, the service will check to see if any new up dates are available. If any updates are available, it will then proceed to download those updates. You will then be notified by an icon in the notification area (near the clock in the bottom right-hand corner of the screen) letting you know that new updates have been downloaded and are ready to be installed. You can then click on it if you're ready to install the updates. Alternatively, when you go to shut down your computer, if there were updates downloaded that haven't been installed, you will see a shield over the "power" button on the "Start" menu. Selecting this will do just that... it will install the updates and then shut off your computer. I like this option because I don't have to have my computer on all the time and it gives me more control over the updates. But at the same time, really no effort is needed.

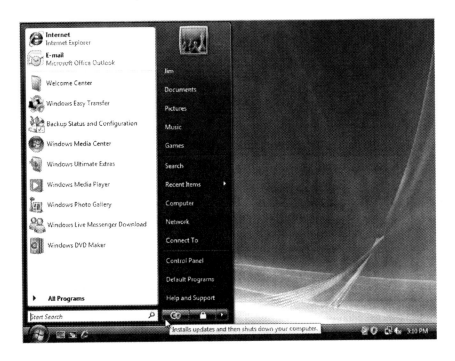

o **Check for updates but let me choose whether to download and install them** - Instead of just being notified that there are updates ready to install, it will notify you to ask if it's OK to download the updates. Then it notifies you again to ask if it's OK to install the updates. I'm not sure why you wouldn't want to download the updates. I don't see too many occasions where you would select this option instead of the previous option, except maybe if you had a slow Internet connection and didn't want to waste bandwidth with the download while you are working on something else. Nevertheless, it's nice that Microsoft does give you other options such as this.

o **Turn off Automatic Updates** - This is highly NOT recommended unless you know you will be going to the Microsoft Update site on a regular basis to check for updates yourself. There are many times when a critical problem is found that can cause major problems and Microsoft quickly releases a fix for it. If you have Automatic Updates turned on, you're in relatively good shape. If you've selected this one, I hope that you're keeping up with this stuff or you may end up with a computer where Windows needs to be completely reinstalled.

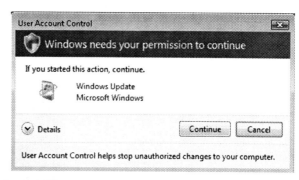

- After making your selection and clicking "OK," if prompted, click "Continue" or enter the administrator credentials to save your changes.

By making these changes and choosing the option that makes the most sense for you, you can help ensure that your installation of the Windows Vista operating system stays current with updates against found vulnerabilities.

In addition to patches from Microsoft, you will want to dig around on the other software you have installed to see how updates are provided and some of the configuration choices you have. This can generally be found by clicking on an "options" or "preferences" menu item of many programs.

chapter 15

Password Protection

Let me start by saying that I am firmly against saving your passwords through the Internet Explorer web browser. You may remember seeing this prompt at some point...

My biggest problem is that when you click "Yes," the Internet Explorer browser puts this password in the registry. The registry is a place where almost all Windows operating system settings are stored. As a side note, the registry is also something you don't want to mess with unless you know what you're doing because one wrong change in the registry can render your computer useless.

Yes, the Windows OS encrypts the passwords, but with a very weak encryption method that can be decrypted by many hack tools... many that are even free to download. Also, there are utilities available to read what the asterisks (or dots) that appear in the password field really are. So if someone got access to your computer and was able to log in as you, they not only have access to the data on your computer, but they can easily have access to every password to every website you've stored on the computer. And that's scary! Think of things you have access to on some websites that you log into and tell me that shouldn't be a reason to not use this. This is especially true of laptops - more and more laptops are being stolen every year.

Too many people have one or two passwords that they use for just about everything. And in most cases, those passwords are not very complex. This poses two problems:
  • By having a password that is not very complex, it is much more likely that your password can be cracked by a hacker, giving access to anything that website has to offer, including all your account information (maybe even your credit card information!).
  • If your passwords are the same for almost all websites you access, if your password is cracked, the hacker now has access to any website where they think you may have an account.

One of the best ways to overcome both of these problems is to use a password management utility. These do a much better job of storing and managing your passwords and they will encrypt the data much more effectively. Most work like this... you set one "master" password to access all your passwords. This is the only password you'll need to remember anymore, so you want to make it somewhat complex. From there, you can create new entries for each website you access - putting in user names, passwords, website addresses, and more. Most of these utilities give you the ability to auto-generate a complex password if desired. They usually also let you copy your account information to the clipboard and paste it into the correct field on the website. And remember that this password file is encrypted... if anyone got access to your password file, he or she cannot access your passwords unless they know your master password. Here are two password management utilities that I recommend...

The first is called "Password Keeper" by a developer named Gregory Braun (**http://www.gregorybraun.com**). I added passwords for many different websites to this utility over the years. It enabled me to develop different and complex passwords for each website. It is also very easy to use. I currently have worked my way up to well over 350 unique passwords stored (due to my line of work) and I only need to remember one - the one to get into it. It allowed me to keep the passwords for all of my accounts complex so that they cannot be cracked as easily because I had "Password Keeper" to remember them. It currently retails for around $20 on his website.

Recently, I have decided to try out a different utility, which I have come to love a little more than "Password Keeper." It's called "Access Manager" and is currently available from Citi-Software **(http://www.accessmanager.co.uk)**. "Access Manager" is available in both a "Free Edition" and a "Professional Edition." The "Professional Edition" obviously offers some "extras" that some users may want and currently runs about $25. However, I have been using the "Free Edition" for months now and have found it to cover everything I need. The software is extremely well designed and easy to use. Although I am still a big fan of "Password Keeper," I have migrated my password list to "Access Manager."

Both utilities keep your data encrypted and by keeping your data in a single file (plus a configuration file in "Access Manager"), your passwords can be easily backed up and easily taken with you when you purchase a new computer.

As a side note, if you use one of these utilities, or any other password management utility, be sure to add the actual files where the passwords are stored to your routine backups.

chapter 16

Computer Protection Wrap-Up

You may be thinking to yourself, "Gosh, I can't believe that I would really need all this stuff... it seems like a lot of effort." And I'll tell you - it is a lot of continuous effort. Unfortunately, although the Internet and email provide wonderful benefits, they also bring with them some bad things. Every day, large numbers of new viruses and spyware are released and if you don't protect yourself, you may cause major problems with your computer.

In addition, you can be causing other people problems by leaving your computer unprotected. Your computer can spread viruses to other people and can become what's referred to as a "zombie" computer meaning it can be used, without your knowledge, to attack other computers. So, even if you don't feel the need to protect your computer from problems, please protect it from causing other people problems. Besides, becoming a zombie computer can also slow your computer down as it's working on attacking other computers.

VIII. The Basics of Backups

chapter 17

Backups

Why do I need them?

If you do anything on your computer other than play games and you're not performing backups, then this chapter's definitely for you. If you lost everything on your computer... documents, email, pictures, music, financial data, etc., would this be a big deal to you? I'm guessing you're thinking something along the lines of "Well, if I lost my [fill this in yourself], it wouldn't be so bad, but if I lost my [fill this in yourself], I'm not sure what I'd do!"

If you think that's dead on, you had better be backing up your data. I don't care how well you think you're maintaining your computer, problems such as hard drives going bad or malicious viruses deleting files are actually relatively common occurrences. Or, what if, God forbid, a fire took place? Would you lose everything?

Backups are critical. How you decide to back up your data should be based a lot on just how long you could be down without access to your data. You may decide that downtime is not that big of a deal to you. Downtime is the time your computer is not available while it is being rebuilt or restored. If that's the case and downtime is not that big of a deal, you might only need to back up certain files to a CD or DVD. On the other hand, if you're running a business and "time is money," then you will need to consider something more elaborate that includes backing up everything, including the Windows operating system, and making it disaster recovery friendly to allow you to be up and running again in just a couple of hours.

I will go into some of the different ways of backing up your data, but whichever method you choose, be sure to always keep the backup media (CD, DVD, external drive) somewhere other than the location of your computer. It's nice to have the data handy, but if a disaster should happen and you end up losing everything in the room where the computer was located, you'll be glad the backup was stored elsewhere. Take it to work, see if Aunt Patty will let you keep a copy at her house - just take it somewhere that is convenient for you, yet keeps it out of your home or home office. A good rule of thumb is to never store data within 15 miles of your backup. That way, if a tragedy were to strike a whole area, you would still most likely be able to get your data back. That may seem extreme, but it can and has happened - look at disasters such as 9/11 in New York and Washington DC or Hurricane Katrina in New Orleans. I hope that you're not involved in something like this, but if your data is critical and something does happen, you'll likely be able to quickly recover.

Let's talk about some feasible options to use for backups for the home or home office user...

External drives

Becoming very popular recently are external drives, particularly USB drives. Because of this popularity, we'll focus specifically on USB drives, but please note that there are other kinds of external drives, such as FireWire. USB (Universal Serial Bus) is just a type of connection to connect an external device to your computer. It has gained tremendous popularity because it is hot-pluggable (meaning you can connect or disconnect the USB device without having to first shut down the computer), it's fast (12 Megabits per second), and it's simple for any user to hook up. Any new local printers you buy generally get connected to your computer using USB. Most digital cameras allow you to connect them to your computer using a USB cable. USB drives themselves are also fairly compact - many comparable to the size of a paperback book.

Like computer hard drives, USB drives continue to come out with the ability to hold more and more data. It's not uncommon to find hard drives that will hold 500 GB anymore - that's slightly more data than you could fit onto 730 CDs! In addition, many USB drives are powered directly by your computer over the USB cable, so you don't need a separate power adapter for it - you just connect the USB cable from the drive to your computer and you're ready to go.

Once you've connected an external USB drive to your computer it will show up as a hard drive on your computer. So if you were to open up "Computer (located by default on the "Start" menu)," you would see the USB drive there and could open files on it and add or delete data. This makes it simple to work with.

The Good:
- **Capacity** - It's hard to find any other medium that will hold 500 GB for only a couple hundred dollars.
- **Simple** - You plug it in and can back up data to it on regular intervals without having to worry about remembering to put a DVD in or anything like that.

The Bad:

- **Location** - Generally, you would just leave this type of drive plugged in and perform backups to it. If a catastrophe happened where the room in which your computer is located burned down, chances are your backup went with it. You could have two drives and swap them out daily, taking one to a different location, but you lose a little bit of the portability you would have with something like CDs or DVDs.
- **One Basket** - Again, since most people would only have one external drive, if something were to happen with the drive (it died or you dropped it), you've just lost all of your backups.

If you're interested in using an external hard drive, these can be found for fair prices at a local Best Buy or Circuit City type of store or a reputable dealer online.

CDs/DVDs

Most everyone should be familiar with CDs and DVDs due to their popularity for listening to music or watching movies. In case you didn't know, there are types of CDs and DVDs that allow you to write your own data to them. Each has certain capacities and abilities. CDs can provide up to a 700 MB capacity. DVDs have capacity ranges that depend on their type which can provide anywhere from 4.7 GB (almost 7 times the capacity of a CD) all the way up to Blu-ray® dual-layer high-definition DVDs which will provide up to 50 GB (the capacity of over 73 CDs!).

CDs - The Good:

- **Inexpensive** - The best part of using basic CDs that can be burned once (CD-Rs) is that they are cheap. Many times, you can find them for next to nothing after rebates.
- **Compact** - Carrying a CD to an offsite location is probably a little easier than carrying an external hard drive (although the drives are becoming smaller!)

CDs - The Bad:

- **Capacity** - A CD can only hold 700 MB. In today's age where storage has become cheap, 700 MB is next to nothing. Chances are you would only be able to back up a small percentage of your data on one CD.
- **Complexity** - If you want to take data and burn it to a CD, that's one thing. However, it can be hard to find good backup software that will burn automatic backups to a CD. And if you do find good software that does it, you still have to remember to change out the CDs each time you have the backup scheduled to run

DVDs - The Good:

- Capacity - With the new dual-layer DVDs offering a 50 GB capacity, you can store quite a bit of data on it.
- Compact - Carrying a DVD to an offsite location is the same as carrying as a CD which is easier than carrying an external hard drive.

DVDs - The Bad:

- **Burners** - Most new computers have optional DVD burners on them and the basic ones will soon become standard on most models. However, with new formats like Blu-ray Discs and HD DVD® with the high definition capacities, the DVD burners that support these will keep the price from dropping too quickly.
- **Capacity** - Capacity makes it as both a good and bad point. I mentioned that the new dual-layer DVDs offer up to a 50 GB capacity, which is ample for many users. However, it will soon seem like nothing a couple years down the line and an alternative means of backup media would likely need to be found.

Online backups

This type of technology is just beginning to mature. Although many vendors have tried unsuccessfully in the past to find a niche in this market, many people are starting to realize the extensive benefits of keeping your data away from your computer.

The idea works by a company offering to house your data on their servers, wherever they might be. In return, you generally pay a monthly fee. So, instead of buying a product, you are in essence, buying a service.

The successful companies are the ones that are able to provide a simple, seamless experience in getting the data from point A to point B. Many have software that you install on your computer that makes a drive show up in "Computer (located by default on the "Start" menu)" that allows you to copy data right to it, similar to an external USB hard drive.

Some of the software the online backup providers provide can be set up to do backups of your important data on regular intervals. In all the reputable companies I've looked into, your data is encrypted securely as it is transferred across the Internet to the provider.

If you should ever need to restore any of the data, you either use their provided software or log into a website. Then you can select what you need and where you want to save it.

As people begin to realize the importance of storing their data in a location away from their computer(s), online backup companies will start to really take off.

The Good:

- **Capacity** - This varies depending on the company you use. With most of the providers, they offer different plans that usually range from 1 GB up to hundreds of gigabytes of storage. And, in almost all cases, the more storage you would like, the greater the cost.
- **Simple** - Most of the providers offer free software with the backup service. This software lets you select what you want backed up, how often, and other options and then takes care of everything for you.

- **Location** - This type of backup makes it easy to ensure that your backups are offsite because as long as you're getting successful backups, the data is already somewhere else. No CDs/DVDs or external hard drives to be taken to another location for storage - everything's electronic making your life a lot easier.

The Bad:

- **Cost** - Unlike an external hard drive, you're paying for a service. And with this service, you should expect that you will be paying a monthly service fee. The prices vary greatly depending on the company you decide to go with, but in almost all cases, it comes down to some type of monthly or annual fee.
- **Speed** - For backups and restores, it will usually be slower than it would be to back up or restore using an external hard drive or CDs/DVDs. This is because you are backing data up across the Internet. However, with many of the companies, once you've backed up your data the first time, only changed files are backed up with later backups. Or, in some cases, the changed file won't be sent, but rather only the actual changes within the file are sent, saving even more bandwidth.
- **Security** - This is probably the biggest concern for the majority of people. The players in the online storage game continue to push security as part of their marketing because they realize that this is one of the biggest things holding many users back from going with this type of service.

The two security pieces involved in these services are the transmission of data across the wide-open Internet and the storage of your personal data on some company's servers. I can tell you that sending data across the Internet seems to be under control by most services. I've looked into several of the online storage companies and they all use a common method of security called Secure Sockets Layer (SSL) to ensure that your data is encrypted using 128-bits of encryption when going from your computer to their servers. Is it possible for someone to intercept your data and be able to overcome the encryption? Yes, but the likelihood is not very high.

What worries me more is that the data is stored on another company's servers. Perhaps you've read about several of the big name companies that have lost private customer information, such as credit card numbers, social security information, etc. I believe the technology used to protect data is very good, but there is always the possibility of human error or human malice that can cause problems. It probably won't happen, but it could. In addition, many people feel more confident in their own abilities to protect things such as their computer data versus some company they don't know.

Here are just some of the online backup companies out there to look into (keep in mind that this is a quick-evolving market, so the prices and plans may change by the time you're reading this):

- **Mozy - http://mozy.com**

Storage	Monthly Rate
2 GB	FREE
Unlimited	$4.95

- **IBackup® - http://www.ibackup.com**

Storage	Monthly Rate
5 GB	$9.95
10 GB	$19.95
50 GB	$49.94

   o There are also plans available that offer point-in-time restores to help attain even more regular backups.

- **Box.net - http://www.box.net**

Storage	Monthly Rate
1 GB	FREE
5 GB	$4.99
15 GB	$9.99

- **MediaMax™ - http://www.mediamax.com**

Storage	Monthly Rate
25 GB	FREE (can only download up to 1 GB per month though)
100 GB	$4.95 (can download up to 10 GB per month)
250 GB	$9.95 (can download up to 25 GB per month)
1000 GB	$29.95 (can download up to 100 GB per month)

   o MediaMax is a newer service of Streamload® and has been strongly improved over the Streamload version.

- **Xdrive® - http://www.xdrive.com**

Storage	Yearly Rate
5 GB	FREE

> o Xdrive was acquired by AOL® in 2005 and has changed this to be a free service, provided you have an AOL account (you can create one for free if you don't already have one).

All said, of the few options I've gone through, I think for most home or home office users, online storage as a service should strongly be considered. Backups are critical. There's no other way to put it. If you're not backing up your data, you will most likely be kicking yourself one day wishing you had been.

On the other side of things, if you're like me and most other people, you don't have the time to sit there and worry about making sure you remember to put a DVD in your computer's burner and taking the backed up copies offsite. Maybe you don't want to think about your external hard drive as being your only computer backup for all your critical data that you leave connected to your computer where it's prone to any home disaster that could happen.

I personally have been using two external hard drives to back up my data on a continuous basis. I have one I keep at my office and one that I keep with my laptop. However, I have recently moved to an online service myself. I like that I can access the data from anywhere using an Internet browser, such as Internet Explorer or Firefox. I like that managing my backups is much simpler for me. I also like that a current copy of all my data will always be offsite somewhere. Without this online service, a fluke scenario could cause me to lose all my data... I bring my laptop to work every weekday. That means during that time, all my data is in one location - my laptop and both external USB hard drives. I could go to lunch one day, come back, and find all my data instantly gone due to a fire at my company.

To me it's not worth it. I've put a lot of work into much of the data that I store on my laptop and the feeling of comfort I get from having a backup with an offsite storage provider is worth the small price it costs me per month. And as a side note, I still use one of my external hard drives to do backups on a less regular basis as well (every month or two) just for convenience and even more peace of mind.

I originally started using the IBackup software to do my backups. However, they made some changes to the service that I disagreed with. They took away the encryption-on-storage option for the plan I had already been using. This ensured that all my data was encrypted at their location - if someone were to get access to that data on their servers, it would be all garbage without the password that only I knew (not even IBackup). Aside from that plan change, the service was fairly good.

However, I have since switched to another service - Mozy. I started using it while it was still in development (beta). It is now out of beta and I am still extremely happy with the service. When I'm not doing anything on my computer for a while, Mozy sees this and takes advantage of the downtime to back up any new or modified files. Because of this, at any point in the day, my backups are almost always close to 100% up to date. The interface is clean and simple and they provide the ability to encrypt data stored on their servers with a password only I know. Mozy is secure and inexpensive and I would definitely recommend at least checking this service out. Again, this is just due to my personal needs. They all have different features and pricing and you will want to investigate the services I mentioned (and quite possibly others) before making a decision as to what would be right for you.

Now, I understand that an online storage service may not be the right option for you as well. Regardless, please think about what would happen if your computer blew up and then find a solution of backing up your data that best caters to your needs.

chapter 18

What Do I Need to Back Up in the Windows Vista OS?

No matter what method of backup you decide to go with, you might be thinking, "I don't know enough about the particulars of computers... how do I know what I need to back up?"

Here's the skinny... in a best-case scenario, it would be great to back up you entire computer, top to bottom. That way, if you ever needed any file(s) restored, you know you have a copy of it. However, that may not always be feasible or, in some cases, the best method to pursue. For instance, if you decided to back up to CD, there's absolutely no way to fit everything on your computer onto one CD. In fact, it would probably take you at the very least three CDs to back up your computer - at the very least! And, the chances of backing everything up to one DVD are probably going to be tough as well. That can add up to be a lot of blank CDs or DVDs being used for your backups.

We'll talk more later about some methods you can use to make sure that you can get a full system backup and be able to get things up and running again quickly. In the meantime, let's go over some of the different things you will probably want to understand and be sure are being backed up.

My recommendation is to back up the following at the very least:
- System State
- Documents
- Contacts/Pictures/Music/Videos/Downloads
- Favorites
- Cookies
- Desktop
- Internet Explorer Passwords
- Microsoft Outlook/Windows Mail settings - accounts, rules, email, contacts, etc.

Let's talk a little bit about each of these...

System State

Depending on what you use to back up your files and folders, you may see something called "System State." The System State is not really a file, but rather a number of files that help make up the state of your computer. The System State is comprised of:
- Registry
- COM+ Class Registration database
- Boot files, including the system files
- System files that are under Windows Resource Protection (WRP)

Some backup utilities will let you specifically check a single box to back up the System State. Because the parts of the System State are so intertwined with one another, you cannot restore individual components of the System State. You must restore the System State as a whole.

Documents

Microsoft decided a long time ago that it makes sense to have a separate, central location for users to store their documents and files, so they created a special folder called "My Documents," that has been around for many years. In the Windows Vista OS, "My Documents" has been renamed simply to "Documents." They've also dropped the "My" from "My Pictures" and "My Music" to now be "Pictures" and "Music."

Many applications use "Documents" as the default open and save location. If you were to go into the Microsoft Word program and then select "File" and then "Open" from the menu, it will show the "Documents" folder first. This is done for consistency. For simplicity, for the remainder of this section, we will refer to the "My Documents" and "Documents" special folders as "Documents."

A "Documents" folder exists for each user profile on a computer. For example, Dave logs into the family computer with the user name "Dave," stores his files in "Documents," and then logs out. Kellie then logs into the same computer with her user name "Kellie." Dave and Kellie each have their own separate

"Documents" folders. By default, Dave cannot easily see Kellie's files in her "Documents" folder and Kellie cannot easily see Dave's files in his "Documents" folder.

In the Windows Vista OS, the default location for the "Documents" folder is on the drive the Windows operating system was installed on (usually the "C" drive) in the user's profile in the "Users" folder. If we continue with the above example, the location of "Documents" would be as follows...

Dave's "Documents" folder in the Windows Vista OS:
    C:\Users\Dave\Documents

And, the default location for Kellie's "Documents" folder would be:
    C:\Users\Kellie\Documents

Contacts/Pictures/Music/Videos/Downloads

The Windows Vista operating system gives each user folders called "Contacts," "Pictures," "Music," "Videos," and "Downloads." "Pictures," "Music," and "Videos" were named "My Pictures," "My Music," and "My Videos" respectively in previous versions of the Windows OS. All these folders function similarly to "Documents" in that a lot of imaging software will look to use "Pictures" as the default open and save locations. The same goes for many music and video software programs, which will do the same with the "Music" and "Videos" folders.

If you store digital pictures, music, or digital home videos on your computer, you will want to check these folders to see if this is the location where the files are stored. Here are the default locations...

Dave's "Pictures" folder in the Windows Vista OS:
    C:\Users\Dave\Pictures

Dave's "Music" folder:
    C:\Users\Dave\Music

Dave's "Videos" folder:
    C:\Users\Dave\Videos

And the default location for Kellie's "Pictures" folder:
    C:\Users\Kellie\Pictures

Kellie's "Music" folder:
    C:\Users\Kellie\Music

Kellie's "Videos" folder:
    C:\Users\Kellie\Videos

The "Contacts" folder is new to the Windows Vista operating system and is a new way of storing exactly that - contact information. This is a change to the Windows Address Book in previous versions of the Windows OS. This can be used by different applications as a centralized way of managing info about friends and family. Here's the default location for your contacts...

> Dave's "Contacts" folder:
>> *C:\Users\Dave\Contacts*

> Kellie's "Contacts" folder:
>> *C:\Users\Kellie\Contacts*

The "Downloads" folder is worth checking to see if you have anything important here that would compel you to back it up as well. Here is the default location for this folder...

> Dave's "Downloads" folder:
>> *C:\Users\Dave\Downloads*

> Kellie's "Downloads" folder:
>> *C:\Users\Kellie\Downloads*

Favorites

When I talk about "Favorites," I'm referring to the "Favorites" listed in the Microsoft Internet Explorer web browser. If you're using a different browser - Mozilla Firefox for instance - your favorites are likely found elsewhere.

Each favorite is actually a single shortcut file. So if in your "Favorites" you have "Yahoo!" listed, there will be a shortcut file named "Yahoo!.url" stored on your hard drive (the .url file extension is hidden by default, however).

Just like "Documents," each user profile has its own separate "Favorites" folder. In our continuing example, the default location of Dave and Kellie's Internet Explorer Favorites would be as follows:

> Dave's "Favorites" folder in the Windows Vista OS:
>> *C:\Users\Dave\Favorites*

> And Kellie's:
>> *C:\Users\Kellie\Favorites*

Cookies

Cookies are probably one of the most misunderstood pieces of computer lingo, besides confusing memory and hard drive space. A cookie is a small text file that is put on your computer by a web server that tells your browser to write to or read from. It's generally used to help customize your online experience. For example, have you ever gone to a web page, such as Yahoo! Mail or Amazon® or whatever, and the website remembers who you are? This might be something like... "Welcome back, Jim... please enter your password." This is due to a cookie on the computer. The first time you go to Yahoo! Mail, Yahoo!'s server asks your web browser (e.g. Internet Explorer) to check for a Yahoo! Mail cookie on the hard drive. If Internet Explorer finds one, it lets the server know the information on it and then the web server can present your stored information. If it doesn't find a cookie, then Yahoo!'s web server will just present a plain web page asking you to log in (no "Welcome back, Jim"). After you log in, if you selected the checkbox that said something like "Remember Me," then Yahoo!'s web server asks your web browser to write a cookie to the hard drive with your user name and password (commonly encrypted by the website). This way, the next time you go to their web page, it can recognize that you're back.

That's it. That's all a cookie does. A cookie is not a virus. Moreover, Yahoo! has access to read from Yahoo!'s cookie only. It cannot read information from a cookie that was stored by Amazon or any other website. On another note, the majority of major websites use cookies and you probably just didn't even know it because they do not need to have a "Remember Me" checkbox - that's only done by web programmers to help give you a choice on their particular website. If you're concerned about cookies, however, they can be shut off by going into the options of your web browser. However, many sites will not work correctly if you have cookies shut off. I would suggest leaving them enabled.

So, if so many websites use cookie technology and they each create their own cookie(s), you would probably have a huge number of these files stored on your computer... right? You got it! I have quite a bit more on my computer than the average user because I keep mine whether I reinstall my laptop or get a new computer. As of right now, I have over 8,000 cookies stored on my hard drive. Remember though, each is very small - in fact, the entire folder of those 8,000 cookies I have is only about 30 Megabytes. Cookies can be a maximum of 4 Kilobytes each... a very small file.

Similar to your favorites, the cookies we're talking about here are for the Internet Explorer browser. All other major web browsers, such as Firefox, support cookies, but they are likely to be stored in different locations.

Internet Explorer browser cookies are also stored in your profile on the hard drive. In the Windows Vista OS, they are stored in a little bit more of an obscure location than most of the other folders we looked at...

The default location where Dave's cookies can be found is:
C:\Users\Dave\AppData\Roaming\Microsoft\Windows\Cookies

And Kellie's are kept in:
C:\Users\Kellie\AppData\Roaming\Microsoft\Windows\Cookies

When Kellie goes to a website, the Internet Explorer browser uses the cookies from her folder and when Dave goes to a website, the browser uses his cookies.

Backing up the cookies on your computer is not critical. However, I'm already backing up my data, so it is not anything difficult to do and is somewhat personable to my computer and me. You may decide otherwise and not back them up - that is completely up to you.

Desktop

You may not have ever thought about it, but everything you store on your desktop is stored in a folder as well. You would think that everything you store on your desktop would be found in your "Documents XE "Documents / My Documents" folder since that is where many people store their files, but it's not. Desktop items are stored in your user profile in a folder named "Desktop."

In the Windows Vista OS, Dave's desktop items are stored in:
C:\Users\Dave\Desktop

And Kellie's desktop items can be found in:
C:\Users\Kellie\Desktop

Any background wallpaper you have is NOT stored in your "Desktop" folder. If you want to back up your wallpaper, you'll need to find out where it's located. It can actually be stored anywhere on the computer, so you may need to search for it by name.

However the default location for wallpaper in the Windows Vista OS is:
C:\WINDOWS\Web\Wallpaper

Public

Keep in mind that because of the profiles, each user that logs into the Windows operating system with a different user name has his/her own documents, favorites, cookies, etc. If Dave logs in and saves something to his desktop, when Kellie logs in, she will not see that on her desktop. They are managed separately in their own profile.

To make things a little more confusing, the Windows Vista OS also has a "Public" profile. In some ways, it is similar to the "All Users" folder in previous versions of Windows operating systems. This folder has items that are shared among users on a computer, including documents, desktop, music, pictures, and video items, among other things. So if Dave had a file that he put in the "Desktop" folder of the "Public" folder, it would show up on Dave's desktop when he logged in and it also would show up on Kellie's desktop when she logged in. However, it's not multiple copies of the file. So if Kellie deleted the file, it deletes it from the "Desktop" folder from "Public," meaning not only is it gone from Kellie's desktop, but it's also gone from Dave's desktop as well. In a nutshell, when you log in, your profile items are a combination of your own profile items, as well as the "Public" items.

The difference between the new "Public" folder in the Windows Vista OS and the "All Users" folder in previous versions of Windows operating systems is that the "Public" folder was designed as a convenient way of file sharing.

Internet Explorer Passwords

As discussed in "Chapter 15 - Password Protection," I am firmly against saving your passwords through the Internet Explorer browser.

However, if you do decide to use the AutoComplete passwords feature in the Internet Explorer browser, you may want to back these up.

These passwords are stored in the registry, not in a folder like "Documents." These are a little trickier to back up. If you are comfortable using the registry, they are all located in:

HKEY_CURRENT_USER\Software\Microsoft\Internet Explorer\IntelliForms\Storage2

This key can be saved as a .REG file to be backed up and then merged into the registry later if ever needed.

If you have no idea what I was just talking about, I'm not going to explain it, because like I mentioned earlier, making a bad change in the registry can leave your computer useless. If you're not sure how to do this, I would recommend using a third-party utility like Rixler Software's "Internet Explorer Password Recovery Master" **(http://www.rixler.com)** to be able to see all your passwords and export them out to a file that can be backed up. If it's later needed, the utility will give you the ability to import the file you had exported.

Windows Mail

Email
If you use the new Windows Mail program in the Windows Vista operating system for email (or newsgroups or RSS feeds), you will probably want to back up your data.

In the Windows Mail program, the default location for storage is:

C:\Users\<User>\AppData\Local\Microsoft\Windows Mail

where <User> is the user name that the profile is found under (Dave or Kellie in our example). The exact path for the Windows Mail client data store can be found by opening the Windows Mail program and selecting the "Tools" menu, then "Options," then clicking on the "Advanced" tab, clicking on "Maintenance," and finally clicking on the "Store Folder" button.

Email Account Settings

Another thing that will make your life a little easier is to back up your email settings. This includes all the connection information on how to connect and download your email. Here's how to do this in the Windows Mail client...

Open up the Windows Mail program, go to the "Tools" menu, and select "Accounts". You'll most likely be concerned mainly with the "Mail" section. For each mail account listed, you will want to click on it and then click on the "Export" button.

You will then be shown the basic save dialog box that asks you where you would like to export the information. My recommendation is to save it in a folder within "Documents" since you will be backing up that folder as part of your backup routine. This may even be the default location it will want to save to. If not, click on the arrow next to "Browse Folders" and then click "Documents" along the left hand side.

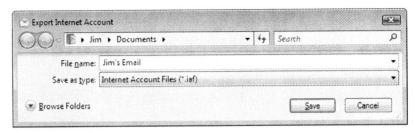

Then click on the "New Folder" icon to allow you to create a new folder. A new folder will then appear in that directory highlighted with the words "New Folder."

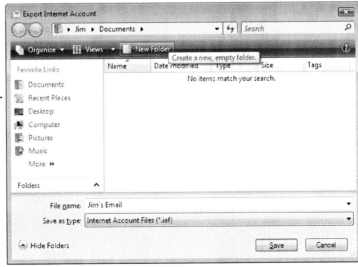

135

Type in a name you would like this folder to be called (maybe "Windows Mail Accounts") and then hit the "Enter" key, which should rename the folder and automatically open it.

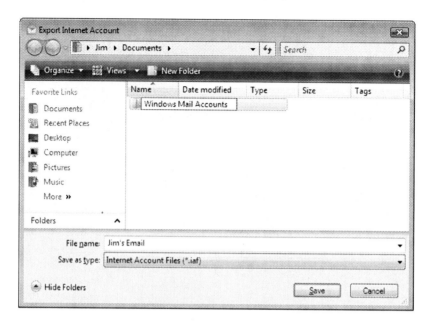

Save the file with a name to describe what it is. In my case, I only have one email account, so the default of "Jim's Email" is good enough for me to remember. I will however append today's date to the end of the filename. If I need to export the same account at a later date - maybe because some information for the email account changed, I will again export the modified account out with the date in the filename. By doing it this way, if I later need to import the settings back in, I can easily look at the file, see when each was created, and then be sure to import the correct one.

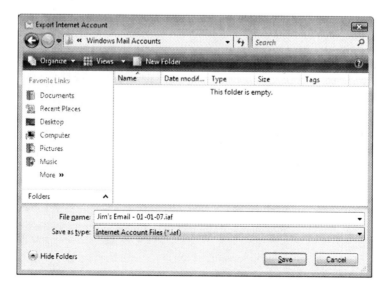

You will then want to save any other accounts that you use in the Windows Mail client. With each account, click on it, click the "Export" button, and then save it in the new folder that you created in "Documents" so all your accounts in the Windows Mail program are in one place.

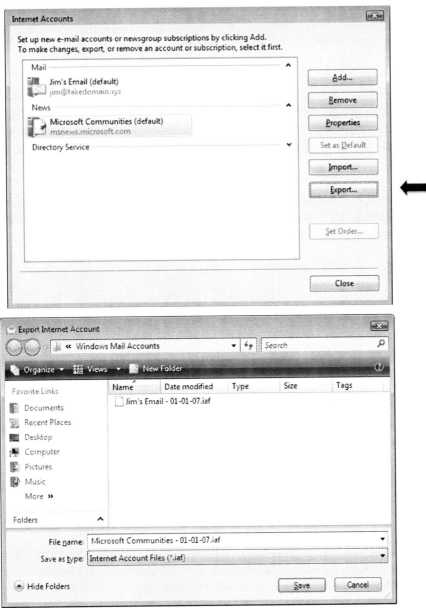

Any time you add a new account or modify the settings of a current account, you will want to do this export procedure so you will always have the current account information saved out in the event that you need it.

Contacts (Address Book)

Almost certainly as important as your email accounts is backing up your Windows Contacts, which are address book entries for the Windows Mail program and some other applications.

Good news... the Windows Mail client uses the Windows Vista operating system Contacts discussed earlier in the chapter, so as long as you back this up, you're covered!

Rules

The Windows Mail email client allows you to create rules to help automate certain things. For instance, you can easily create a rule to say that if an email comes from your Uncle Dennis' email address, then automatically put it into a folder you created called "Family." You may create a rule that will automatically forward a copy of the email to everyone in a particular group if it has something like the words "Business Meeting" in the subject.

If you have created a number of message rules in the Windows Mail client, you may want to include these as part of your backup so you don't have to recreate each of them. Unfortunately, Microsoft didn't create an easy way to back up your rules. If you're comfortable using the registry, you can go to:

HKEY_CURRENT_USER\Software\Microsoft\Windows Mail\Rules\Mail

You can then save out the above key to a .REG file to be backed up, which can then be merged into the registry later if ever needed.

If you have rules for newsgroups, those can be found in:

HKEY_CURRENT_USER\Software\Microsoft\Windows Mail\Rules\News

Just like the message rules for your email, you can save out this key to a .REG file that can then be merged into the registry later if ever needed.

Once again, if you're not sure what I'm talking about with the registry, I'm not going to go into detail because making a bad change in the registry can leave your computer completely dead in the water.

Other Info

If the above information on backing up rules seems a little bit too much or you'd just like another option, you might want to look at **http://www.abf-soft.com**. The company, ABF software, Inc., currently offers a tool called "ABF Outlook Express Backup" that will allow you to not only easily back up the Outlook Express client rules, but everything we've talked about and more. With it, you can back up your email messages, your address book, your account settings, rules you've created, any blocked senders you've added, email signatures, and stationeries you may have created. As I write this, the Windows Mail client is still brand new, but I would be willing to bet that ABF Software will soon expand this utility to support

Windows Mail. The Outlook Express version currently runs about $30, but that small amount of money may save you many headaches. And, you can try it free for 30 days to decide if it's something that's worth it to you.

Microsoft Outlook 2007

The Microsoft Outlook messaging client is like the Outlook Express or Windows Mail email client on steroids. It does not come with the Windows OS, however. Most users get the Microsoft Outlook software when they purchase certain versions of the Microsoft Office suite, but it can also be purchased by itself.

Don't get confused by the name - Microsoft Outlook and Outlook Express are like two different animals. Although the Microsoft Outlook software provides the same general functionality as the Outlook Express and Windows Mail clients (and more!), the insides are quite a bit different. I have a feeling the marketing department at Microsoft realized they shouldn't have named the two so similarly, which may have contributed to the new name for the Windows Mail client.

In this section, I'll be concentrating on the Microsoft Outlook 2007 software (the newest version of the Microsoft Office suite).

Email
The Microsoft Outlook messaging client allows you to connect to a Microsoft Exchange server via a technology called MAPI. It also allows you to connect to email servers via POP3, IMAP, etc. If you are connecting to an Exchange server, your mail is most likely be stored on the server itself with maybe a cached copy on your desktop/laptop. This method is usually used with small businesses up through large enterprises. In this case, your email is usually (and hopefully!) being backed up at the server level. The same goes for IMAP accounts in which the mail is stored on the email server, but cached on the email client. We'll be focusing on email accounts that use POP3 where email is downloaded and usually stored on the client. Most home and home office email providers are set up to use POP3.

When you set up the the Microsoft Outlook (without Microsoft Exchange) program, it is set up to store your all your email and some settings in a single file with an extension of .PST. PST files are Personal Folders files. This makes it a little easier to back some things up. In the Windows Vista OS, the default location is:

C:\Users\<User>\AppData\Local\Microsoft\Outlook

To verify where the PST for your email is stored:

1. <u>Right-click</u> on the top-level node in the Outlook client, which by default has the name "Personal Folders,"

2. Select "Properties for <Personal Folders>," where "Personal Folders" is the name of the top-level node.

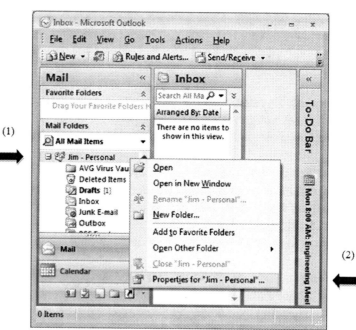

(Outlook 2007)

3. Select the "Advanced" button.

(Outlook 2007)

4. Look at the line that says "Filename" to find out the location of your PST file.

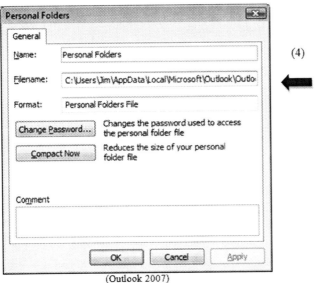

(Outlook 2007)

In the Outlook 2007 software screenshot, the PST file is located in the default location:

C:\Documents and Settings\[User Name]\Local Settings\Application Data\Microsoft\Outlook"

with a filename of "Outlook.pst"

Wherever your filename location is pointing to, that's the file that you will want to back up - it contains all your email as well as most of your personalized settings.

Email Account Settings

Your account settings consist of the different email setup configurations. This includes how you are able to have the Microsoft Outlook client connect to the mail server where you get your email. This is usually via a connection protocol called POP3 that allows you to download your email (generally from your ISP).

Here's some good news... unlike the Windows Mail client, your account settings are stored as part of your PST file (as discussed above). By backing up your PST, you're automatically taking care of backing up your account settings.

Contacts (Address Book)

With older versions of the Microsoft Outlook program (98 and earlier), your personal address book was a separate file than your PST file. However, with current versions of the Outlook software (2000 and higher), your address book information is stored as Outlook Contacts. This actually makes things simpler when talking about backups because, again, by default, your Contacts are stored in your PST. Therefore, backing up your PST file will also take care of backing up your Contacts.

Rules

As I mentioned with the Windows Mail client, rules help automate certain things. For example, you can create a rule to say that if an email comes from your Uncle Dennis' email address then automatically put it into a folder you created called "Family" and will send a reply back to Uncle Dennis letting him know you got his email.

Here's some more good news... any rules you have are also stored in your PST file (with the Microsoft Outlook 2002 software and higher).

Some Important PST File Key Points

Wow, this is getting to be easy for the the Microsoft Outlook client - so far, we know that we just need to back up our PST file to get our email, email settings, Contacts, and rules. Your PST file also includes your calendar items, tasks, and notes that you create in Outlook.

AutoArchive

Now, here's something important that you will want to keep in mind. Microsoft has a feature called "AutoArchive" that it put in the Outlook software. The idea is that, by default, it will move all email that is older than 6 months to a separate PST for archive purposes. The default settings can be changed from archiving to simply deleting the emails and the time of 6 months can be set to something that makes more sense for you as well. It can also be set up to be just for specific folders. I think it's kind of a cool feature to include.

The problem is that it's turned on by default. You now have to be careful because everything I said about backing up your PST file to save out everything is only partially true. With this turned on, you also have to take into consideration this additional "archive" PST.

By default, in the Windows Vista operating system, it's stored in:

C:\Users\<User Name>\App Data\Local\Microsoft\Outlook\Archive.pst

I always turn this off before I start using the Outlook software. You can see if it's turned on by going into the Outlook client and doing the following:

1. Click on the "Tools" menu and selecting "Options." Then go to the "Other" tab and click on the "AutoArchive" button.

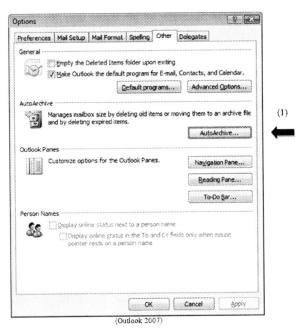

(1)

(Outlook 2007)

2. You can adjust the settings if you want or you can shut it off completely. To shut it off, just uncheck the "Run AutoArchive every <14> days" checkbox and then click "OK."

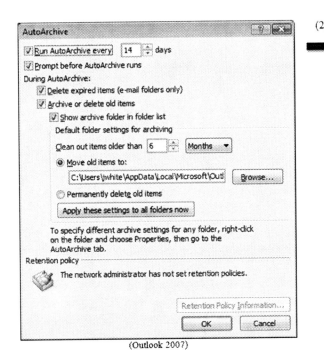

(Outlook 2007)

(2)

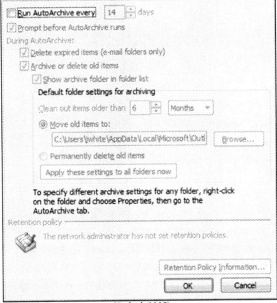

(Outlook 2007)

It's up to you whether or not you want to leave this on or turn it off, but here's why I always shut it off on my computer and computers I set up for friends and family.

1. As I said before, you've now just added another item you need to make sure you add to your backup and this one can be easily forgotten!
2. If you ever need to refer to an older email, you need to open this file to even get to it. Why not just set up folders in the Outlook client for organization and sort by date if need be? You can easily right-click on any folder and select "New Folder..." to add a folder under it.

If you've been using the Microsoft Outlook software for a while and now want to stop using the "AutoArchive" feature, shut it off as described above. Be sure to first take note of "Move old items to" path that is shown in the settings. After shutting it off, you then have two choices - either back up the archive PST file at least one time and leave the data there or take the mail data out of the archive PST file and put it back into your main PST file. I would recommend the latter so you can keep everything together.

To do this, you will want to open the Outlook program and go to the "File" menu and select "Open" and then "Outlook Data File..." The default location that opens will most likely have your "AutoArchive" PST file showing ("archive.pst"). If not, browse to the location that you noted when you turned off the "AutoArchive" feature. Select the file and open it.

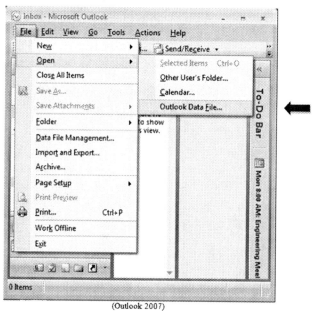

(Outlook 2007)

You will now see both files open in the mail folders hierarchy in the left pane. Now you just need to select and drag any email messages you want back in your main PST from your archive PST. Once you're done with that, you can right-click on the top-level node of the archive PST and select "Close <Personal Folder>." That's it... now you no longer need to worry about the Microsoft "feature" anymore.

Unicode PST files

The Outlook 2003 software introduced a new type of PST file called a Unicode-capable PST file. The only thing you need to care about with this new format is that it can hold a lot more information. Previously, non-Unicode PSTs had a 2-Gigabyte limit. This caused problems if you did actually hit that limit - sometimes to the point where you could lose some of the information that was actually in it. The new Unicode-capable PST overcomes this limit. Unless you plan to access your Outlook software data with a version of Outlook software older than Microsoft Outlook 2003, then I would recommend that you ensure you are using the new format. The non-Unicode PSTs may also be an exception to shutting off the "AutoArchive" feature. If you have this old-style PST format and are close to the 2-Gigabyte limit, the "AutoArchive" may be helping keep you within the limit.

To see which type of PST file you are using...

1. Right-click on the top-level node in the Outlook client, which by default has the name "Personal Folders,"

(1)

2. Select "Properties for <Personal Folders>," where "Personal Folders" is the name of the top-level node.

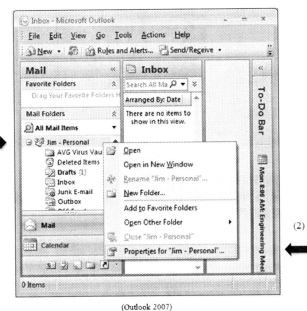

(2)

(Outlook 2007)

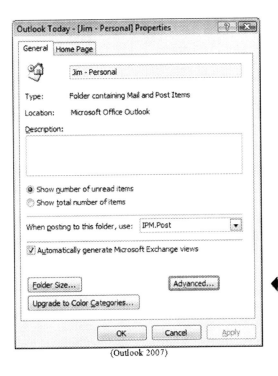

(3)

3. Select the "Advanced" button.

(Outlook 2007)

4. Look at the line that says "Format." If it says "Personal Folders File (97-2002)," then you have the older non-Unicode format.

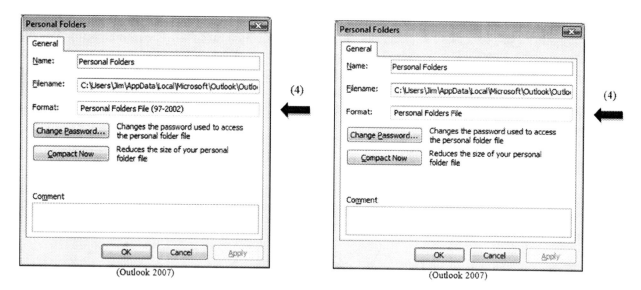

(Outlook 2007)   (Outlook 2007)

In the first screenshot, the PST file is using the old non-Unicode format, while the second screenshot shows the Outlook 2007 client using the new Unicode PST format (no "97-2002" following the words "Personal Folders File."

Unfortunately, if you have the older style PST format and want to convert it to the newer format, there's no conversion utility to do this. You will need to create a new PST in the newer format and then import everything in from your old-style PST. For more information on how to do this, look at the Microsoft article "Convert a non-Unicode data file (.pst) to a Unicode data file (.pst)," currently located at: **http://office.microsoft.com/en-us/assistance/HP01038351 1033.aspx**

I've spent quite a bit of time discussing the Microsoft Outlook software because many people who use it as a personal information manager begin to strongly rely on the data that is in it and would be devastated if they lost this information.

On that note, the last thing I would like to mention is that Microsoft has released an add-in for the Outlook 2000 application and higher called "Outlook 2003/2002 Add-in: Personal Folders Backup." It works for the Outlook 2007 software as well.

It backs up your PST file to a location you specify at regular intervals (which you also specify). If you are already backing up your PST, this just adds a level of protection. For example, let's say you're backing up your PST file with your backup on a weekly basis - every Sunday. You also use the add-in to back up your PST file on a daily basis. Then on one particular Friday, you begin having a problem with Outlook not working due to your PST file being corrupt and unfixable. Well, you now have a couple choices. You can restore your PST from Sunday's backup, which would mean you would lose any email, calendaring information, etc. that was sent, received, or entered into the Outlook client from the time of Sunday's backup all the way through Friday. If you're using the Microsoft utility, however, your other option is to simply try to use the last daily PST backup - which might be Thursday, but also might even be Friday depending on when it ran. It may or may not be successful - depending on when the corruption occurred - but, if it does, you just saved a good 4 or 5 days of lost data!

More information on downloading and using this free add-in can be found by looking at "Back up Outlook data with the Microsoft Outlook Personal Folders Backup tool," currently located at **http://www.microsoft.com/downloads/details.aspx?FamilyID=8b081f3a-b7d0-4b16-b8af-5a63 22f4fd01&DisplayLang=en**

However, that's a lot to have to type into your browser... you might be able to get to it a little quicker by going to the Google search engine (**http://www.google.com**) and typing in some or all of the name of the tool: "Outlook 2003 Add-in: Personal Folders Backup."

Summary of the files to back up

I know this is a long chapter, but it is probably also one of the most critical to ensuring that you are backing up data that is important to you, so I'm glad you made it through it.

To help sum up, here are some of the things I recommend backing up...

- System State
- Documents
- Contacts/Pictures/Music/Videos/Downloads
- Favorites
- Cookies
- Desktop
- Internet Explorer Passwords
- Windows Mail
  - o Email
  - o Email Account Settings
  - o Contacts
  - o Rules
- Microsoft Outlook
  - o PST file - If set up correctly, your PST file will contain your Email, Email Account Settings, Contacts, and Rules

The list above is by no means an all-inclusive list of things that should be backed up, but it should encompass many of the most common. Take the information provided and use it as a foundation to build from. Leave out anything that may not apply to you and then add things to it that take into the account what you are using.

For example, if you are using the Intuit Quicken financial software, check within the help contents (go to the "Help" menu and then select "Quicken Help"). Go to the Index and start typing "backing up your data." You will see a number of topics that will help you to understand what you need to back up.

If you don't find information in the software's help file, check the version of the software you are running by going to the "Help" menu and selecting "About..." The majority of software lets you determine the version you are using with a "Help" and "About" menu item. Then go to the vendor's website (in our case **http://www.quicken.intuit.com**) and click on "Help & Support." When you select the version of the software you're running, you can see "hot topics" listed such as "Tell me about backing up or restoring my Quicken data file." If you don't see it listed there, try doing a search for "backup data" in the support area's search box.

Finally, if that doesn't seem to work, utilize a good search engine like Google web search (**http://www.google.com**) to try to find out how to back it up. In this case, I would type "quicken 2007 backup data" into the search box. Chances are you will find some good information that way. Keep in mind though, that not everyone on the Internet is out to give you good advice. Try to keep an open mind to what you read because you'll find a lot of helpful tips, but also be cautious when following the information you got from "Joe's Auto-Body Shop and Software Support." In addition, sometimes in the software arena, if the Google search doesn't present you with satisfactory results, you may want to try the Google Groups™ discussion forums (**http://groups.google.com**). These are question and answer forums for every topic under the sun. Some are managed by professionals and some are not, but you may find something to point you in the right direction.

Another example of software not mentioned might be something like the Mozilla Firefox web browser. Recently a very large number of people have started using the Mozilla Firefox browser in place of, or in addition to, the Internet Explorer web browser. Your favorites, cookies, passwords, etc. are stored in a completely different location than in the Internet Explorer browser. If you are using the Firefox browser, you'll want to investigate where the files/folders are located that would need to be backed up. As a head start, more information can currently be found by going to **http://www.mozilla.org/support/firefox/profile**. This site discusses where to find your profile (cookies and favorites included).

The next few chapters will tell you how to create different types of backups using the built-in Windows Backup. Remember, this is not your only choice, but just an option to consider.

chapter 19

Windows Backups

You now need to decide how to back up your files. This is just as important of a question as what files to back up. If you decide to use an online backup solution, be sure the solution you choose has software that you can use to automate your backups. If not, you may want to find out why not - if you're paying for online storage only, that's one thing. Nevertheless, if you're paying for a service, a solid backup software solution should be a part of it.

Regardless of the type of backup you are doing, I would strongly recommend closing all applications while your backup is running, such as the Microsoft Outlook or Windows Mail client. It will ensure that the backup utility has full access to your files and the memory that the applications use will be freed up for the backup utility to use if necessary.

The key to the next couple of chapters is going to be that both the files that need to be backed up, as well as the destination that the files will be backed up to, are shown as drives or network shares on your computer. This can be found by looking in "Computer" (found by default on the "Start" menu).

Please note that if you are using certain types of backup solutions (such as some online solutions), this may not apply. Some backup solutions may just let you choose what to back up and then it handles the destination information on its own. However, the next few chapters will be dealing specifically with the built-in Windows Vista OS backup utilities.

Windows Backup

Different versions of Windows Backup have been built into the Windows operating system for many years now. While there are many critics that will disagree with my thinking, I have a tendency to like things that are built right in by Microsoft because if a problem occurs with the built-in program, it's usually easier to troubleshoot what the cause is. For instance, if we were using a third-party backup utility and started having problems backing things up, the software vendor might start you off in the direction of asking you if you experience the same problem backing things up with Windows Backup. That's because some vendors will build their backup software based off the capabilities of Windows Backup. You're then stuck troubleshooting an extra layer.

The new version of Windows Backup has been completely rebuilt in the Windows Vista operating system. It's now more user-friendly to help ensure that backups are set up quickly and correctly. It also gives you more choices of what devices to back up to than what was available in previous versions of the Windows OS. Here's how to configure a Windows Backup in the Windows Vista OS...

Please note that you must be logged in with an administrator account in order to be able to configure backups in the Windows Vista OS.

To open Windows Backup, click on the "Start" button, then go to "Programs" or "All Programs" (depending on how your "Start" menu is set up), then go to "Accessories," "System Tools," and then select "Backup Status and Configuration."

The main screen for backups and restores is shown. If this is the first time you're using the program, it will look like this...

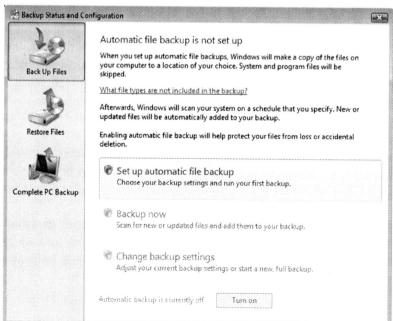

You now have a couple of options for backing up your computer...

"Complete PC Backup" Versus "Back Up Files"

If you have plenty of capacity (like a large external hard drive), I would strongly recommend that you first select "Complete PC Backup" to perform an initial backup. The "Complete PC Backup" option will do just that - it will create a backup of your entire computer. In the event of a serious Windows problem, you can boot from the Windows Vista operating system DVD (or from the restore partition in some cases) and restore the last good backup without the need to do an entire reinstall of Windows. When you perform your first backup as a Complete PC Backup, it will back up everything on your computer. The good news is that if you later perform another Complete PC Backup, it will just be backing up changes. Because of that, the size of this next backup (and all subsequent backups) will likely be a lot smaller. This will help save some disk space.

In addition to the above benefits, the Complete PC Backup gives you the ability to actually perform the entire restore (Windows OS and all) to another computer... something that could be used to migrate to a new computer.

Please keep in mind that Complete PC Backup is not available in Windows Vista Home Basic or Windows Vista Home Premium. It also does not provide a "wizard" to schedule the backup directly from in the backup program. I will, however, show you a method to schedule them to run automatically in a different manner in "Chapter 21 - Scheduling a Complete PC Backup Image."

The "Back Up Files" option is more like a traditional backup. It will allow you to choose what types of files to back up, which should help save on drive space. This type of backup allows you to be able to restore specific files if needed later. Unfortunately, however, if the Windows operating system has a major meltdown, a reinstallation of the operating system would probably need to be performed first, then each application would need to be reinstalled, followed by the restore of your backed up files. It will likely be a very long ordeal, but it should still get the job done.

In general, I would recommend that if you have a version of Windows Vista that allows the Complete PC Backup, then perform at least an initial backup using this feature. Then set up a regularly scheduled "Back Up Files" backup to ensure that changes to files are being backed up on a regular basis. Finally, I recommend that you look at scheduling Complete PC Backup images to run weekly - or even daily. That way if your hard drive were to crash or you had a major Windows issue, you could restore your latest Complete PC Backup image to get you back up and running in the least amount of time and then be able to restore necessary data files from your latest "Back Up Files" backup.

In either case, you have some options of what kind of devices you can back up to. Here are some available choices in the Windows Backup and my thoughts:

- Back up to another logical partition on your computer. This is like a division of your physical hard drive. Maybe you have one 80GB hard drive... it may logically partitioned to look like a 20 GB "C" drive and a 60 GB "D" drive. In this example then, you could back up your "C" drive to the "D" drive.

  Pros: Easy to access and back up to... it's always there.

  Cons: All your eggs are in one basket. If your hard drive has physical hardware problems and dies, you not only lost your computer data, but also the backup itself!

- Back up to CD's or DVD's.

  Pros: Keeps your backups on separate media. If the CD's or DVD's of your last backup had problems (like major scratches), you could at least go back to the CD's or DVD's from the backup before.

  Cons: Let's say you are able to pull off just needing one CD or DVD for one backup of your data. That's at bare minimum... so you'll need at least 52 CD's or DVD's to do a year's worth of backups on a weekly basis. Sure, they can usually be found at inexpensive prices, but that's a lot of CD's or DVD's you're going to quickly start accumulating. It also means you'll need to remember to change out the CD's or DVD's between backups and possibly during the backup if more than one disc is required.

- Back up to another internal hard drive.

  Pros: Easy to access and back up to... it's always there. Keeps your backups on a separate location, so if your main hard drive dies, your backups are stored on another drive. You can generally get a large enough drive to cover your backup needs for an inexpensive price.

  Cons: You need to install the other hard drive in your computer (or have someone do it for you) - not a difficult task, but if you shudder at the thought at opening up your computer, then this may be a problem for you. Additionally, if you have a laptop, this may not be an option. Finally, if your computer is involved in som thing like a fire, you're probably losing both your main hard drive and your "backups" hard drive.

- Back up to an external hard drive (i.e. USB or FireWire).

  Pros: These have become inexpensive and are a snap to connect or disconnect from your computer. Keeps your backups in a separate location, so if your main hard drive was to die, your backups are still stored on another drive. You can generally get a large enough drive to cover your backup needs for an inexpensive price.

  Cons: Unless you disconnect and take the external drive offsite on a regular basis, if your computer is involved in a something like a fire, you're probably losing both your main hard drive and your "backups" hard drive.

- Back up to another computer or server. If you have a network in place, you can back up to another computer.

  Pros: Keeps your backups in separate location. Once set up, you are limited only to the drive space on the other computer.

  Cons: You may not have a home network in place. Once again, if your computer is involved in a fire, for instance, there's still a chance you're going to lose both your main hard drive and the computer with your backups.

Honestly, I would recommend backing up to an external hard drive. You can get a considerably large external USB hard drive that should be able to hold your computer backups fairly inexpensively. An up-front cost of $100 or so will seem well worth it when your computer does crash and you can get it back up and running within an hour or so instead of an agonizing day or so. If the thought of keeping your data by your computer is a concern for you, you could always look at getting multiple drives, synchronizing them periodically to ensure the backups are on both drives, and then taking one elsewhere away from your home.

The next couple of chapters will look at creating backups with the Complete PC Backup and then scheduling a Complete PC Backup with the "Task Scheduler." After that, I'll show you how to create and schedule backups with the "Back Up Files" option.

chapter 20.

Creating a Complete PC Backup Image

Creating a Complete PC Backup will ensure that you now have a complete bit-by-bit image of the drive(s) on your computer. This is excellent to have if you have a major Windows OS catastrophe and need to get your computer back to the point it was when the image was created. With a Complete PC Backup image, you can do just that. In an extremely short amount of time, you can get your computer up-and-running exactly how it was when the image was created. A downside to this is that you can only restore the entire drive(s), not individual files. Because of this, you will also ensure that you also create a standard file backup.

Remember that the Complete PC Backup feature is not available in the Windows Vista "Home" editions (Home Basic or Home Premium).

Let's get started on creating a Complete PC Backup in Windows Vista...

To open Windows Backup, click on the "Start" button, then go to "Programs" or "All Programs" (depending on how your "Start" menu is set up), then go to "Accessories," "System Tools," and then select "Backup Status and Configuration."

The main screen for backups and restores is shown...

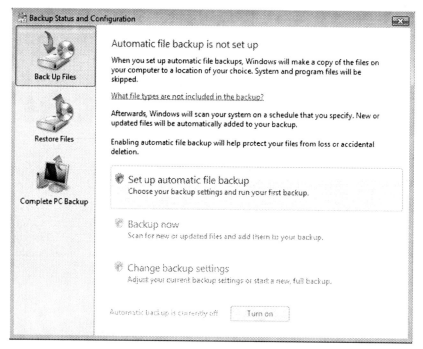

From the main "Backup Status and Configuration" screen, click on "Complete PC Backup" in the left pane. Then click on the "Create a backup now" button.

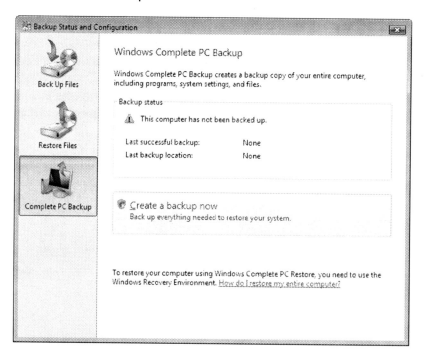

If prompted, click "Continue" to open the backup configuration screen...

On the next screen, you'll select where you would like your backups to be located. In my example, I'll be backing up files to my external USB hard drive that is already set up and turned on. My external hard drive has a drive letter of "G" - yours may be something different. Select the correct location and then click "Next."

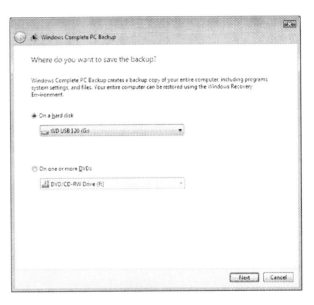

On the next screen, you confirm how your computer will be backed up. If you have more than one drive partition, you can select the ones you would like to back up. The System partition (usually the "C" drive) cannot be unchecked. In my case, I selected the other partitions as well, and will be backing up the "C," "D," and "L," partitions to my external USB drive ("G").

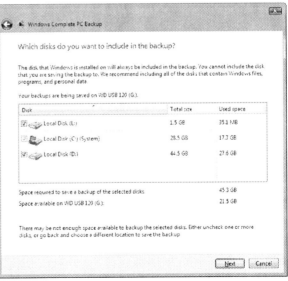

Now simply click on the "Start backup" button and your first full backup will begin...

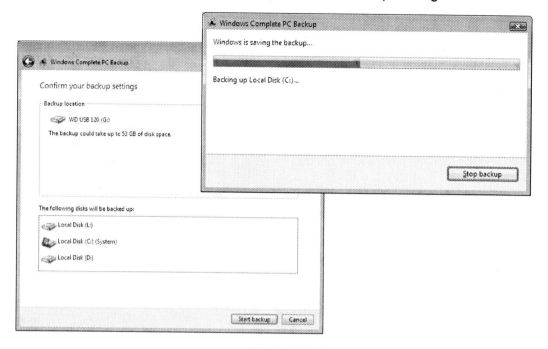

This first backup will likely take longer to run than subsequent backups. When the backup completes, the program will let you know...

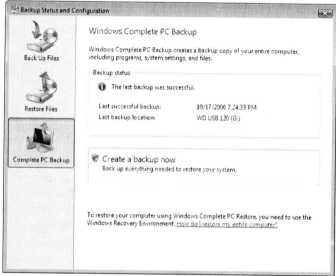

That's all there is to it. When you want to create another Complete PC Backup image at a later time, simply follow the steps above. If there is already an image located in that same location, it will automatically only back up the changes to the image, so it should be considerably smaller and the image creation should be quicker.

chapter 21

Scheduling a Complete PC Backup Image

You may have noticed while working with the Complete PC Backup screens in the previous chapter, there really wasn't an option to update this image file on an automatic scheduled basis. Unfortunately, Microsoft didn't provide a simple way to do this from the "Backup Status and Configuration" screen.

However, it can be done and I would recommend that you do this on a periodic basis. Keep in mind that this type of imaging is not meant to be able to restore individual files. Restoring a Complete PC Backup image will restore the whole computer or selected partitions, including all files. Because of this, you will still want to create and schedule regular file backups for that purpose as discussed in the next chapter, but in the event of a crash, this will provide the possibility of getting your computer back to the way it was in a short amount of time.

In this chapter, I will be backing up to an external USB hard drive connected to my computer. This is generally the simplest and cheapest method to use. There are other options, but these can be a little more complex to set up.

To schedule Complete PC Backup images, we'll be using the "Task Scheduler." Please note that you need to be logged in with an administrator account in order to continue. Also, remember that the Complete PC Backup feature is not available in the Windows Vista Home editions (Basic or Premium).

You can launch the "Task Scheduler" program by clicking on the "Start" button, typing task scheduler in the search box and then pressing the "Enter" key. If prompted for permission, click "Continue."

When the "Task Scheduler" comes up, click "Create Basic Task..." in the "Actions" pane.

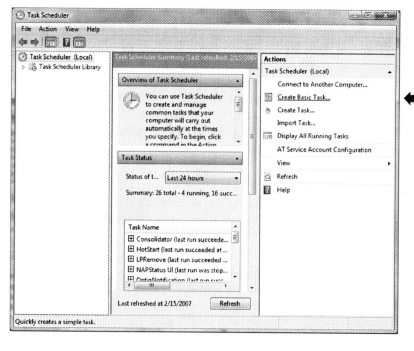

The "Create Basic Task Wizard" will then launch. The first thing you will need to do is give the scheduled task a name. In my example, I'm naming the task "Complete PC Backups." Once you've given the task a name (a description is optional), then click "Next."

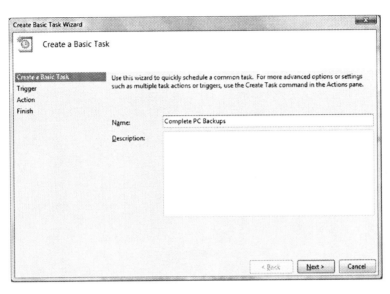

You now need to decide how often you would like the "Complete PC Backups" task to run. The first image that is created will be large and take a while to run because it is an exact copy of everything on your computer. However, subsequent backups will only be backing up the changes that have been made, so the images will be quite a bit smaller and take less time to run. Because of that, if possible, I would recommend scheduling the backups to run daily to keep the image current. Otherwise, choose the option that works best for you. Then click "Next."

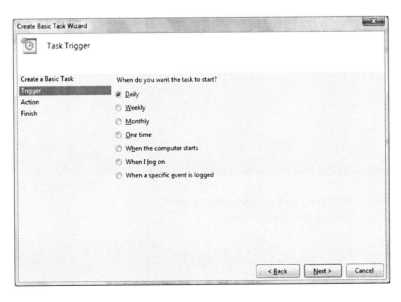

Depending on your previous selection, you may see a different prompt than you shown here. Regardless, enter in the information requested. In my example, I am going to have the backup run at 1:00am every night. As a hint, the computer must be turned on for the backup to run, so if you normally shut your computer off at night, you'll need to choose a different time. After making any necessary adjusts, click "Next" to continue.

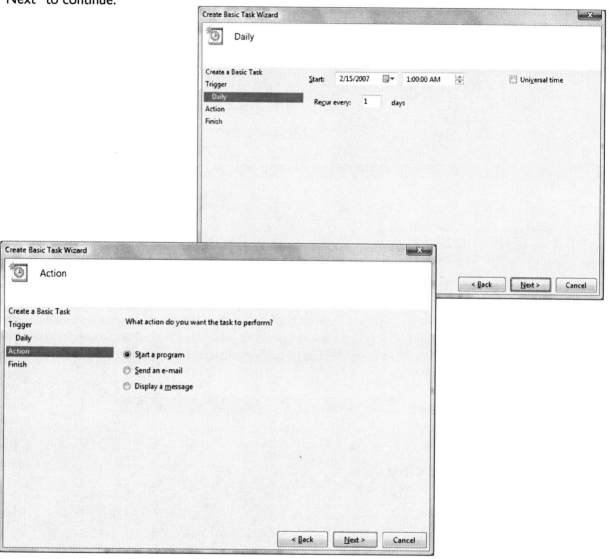

When asked what action you would like to perform, ensure that "Start a program" is selected and click "Next."

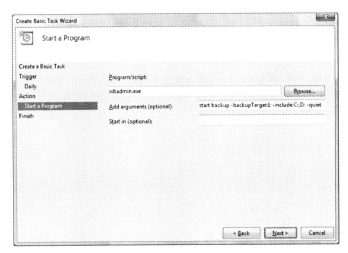

In the "Program/script" textbox, type in **wbadmin.exe** (no need to use the "Browse" button. Then in "Add arguments" box, you need to carefully type the following:

start backup -backupTarget:<DestDrive>: -include:<SourceDrive> -quiet

<DestDrive> will be the letter of the external hard drive you want to back up your Complete PC Backup image to. You'll notice that in my case, the drive letter is "I," so that is what I used.

For <SourceDrive>, you will want to include the drive letter you want backed up on your computer followed by a colon. If you have multiple partitions to back up on your computer, you can separate each with a comma. In almost everyone's case, you will at least have a "C" drive. In my example, I have a "C" and a "D" partition, so I will put in both with a comma separating them.

My complete syntax for "Add arguments" is:

    start backup -backupTarget:I: -include:C:,D: -quiet

Once you've have that information correct, the hard part is over! Go ahead and click "Next" to continue

On the summary screen, be sure to check the box to "Open the Properties dialog for this task when I click Finish" and then click the "Finish" button.

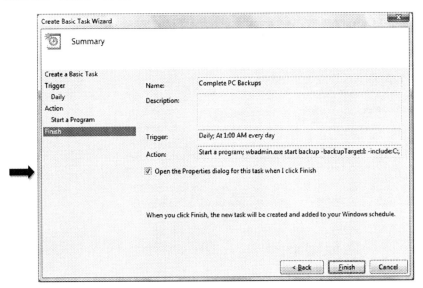

When the properties screen comes up, you will want to check the box for "Run with highest privileges" on the "General" tab. You may also optionally select "Run whether user is logged on or not." If you have more than one user account on your computer and may not always be logged on with the account you are using to create the backup, this will allow the backup to run even if you are not logged on. I would recommend this option. You will, however, be prompted for your password when clicking "OK" here, so be careful to enter it correctly. Once you've made the appropriate change(s), click "OK."

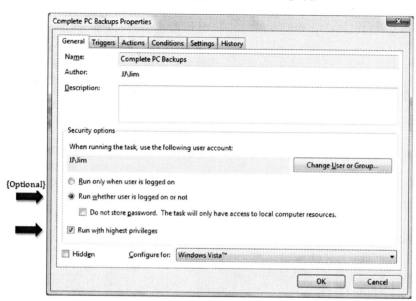

That's it... you've set up your scheduled Complete PC Backup. Now for the decisive moment - we need to test it. To get to it, click on "Task Scheduler Library" in the left pane. Your scheduled task will appear in the middle pane. Right-click on it and you will notice a few options, one of them being "Properties." Remember that option for later - that is how you can get in to modify the job in case you wanted to change the scheduled time to run, for instance. For now, though, you just need to select "Run."

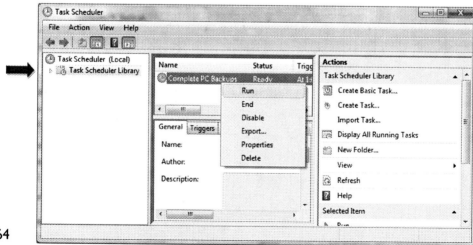

You should see a command prompt window pop up on your screen and the backup will start. If this is the first Complete PC Backup to your external drive, it will probably take a while to run. Just let it run its course...

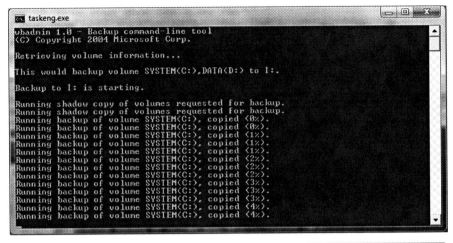

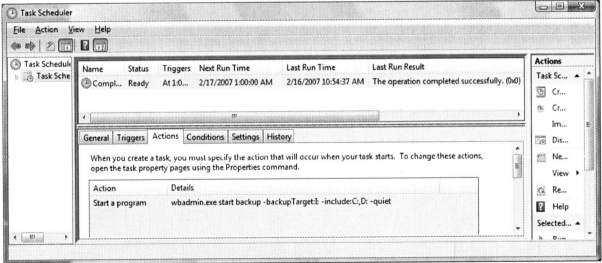

When the backup is complete, the command prompt window will automatically close. To see if the task ran successfully, go back to the "Task Scheduler" and then press the "F5" key to refresh the screen. Look under the column marked "Last Run Result." The message should state, "The operation completed successfully. (0x0)" for your backup task.

If you see a different message, you have likely entered in the incorrect syntax. You'll want to go back through this chapter and make sure everything is 100% correct. If the backup completed successfully... congratulations! You now have a way to get your computer back to this exact point in time should your hard drive go bad or something similar happens.

chapter 22

Creating and Scheduling a Backup Using "Back Up Files"

The "Back Up Files" backup in the Windows Vista OS will help you back up your important files on your computer on a regular basis. This can be used if you lose an important file(s) on your computer due to accidentally deleting it or from something malicious like a virus.

Please note that you must be logged in with an administrator account in order to be able to configure backups in the Windows Vista operating system.

To open Windows Backup, click on the "Start" button, then go to "Programs" or "All Programs" (depending on how your "Start" menu is set up), then go to "Accessories," "System Tools," and then select "Backup Status and Configuration."

The main screen for backups and restores is shown. If this is the first time you're using the program, it will look like this...

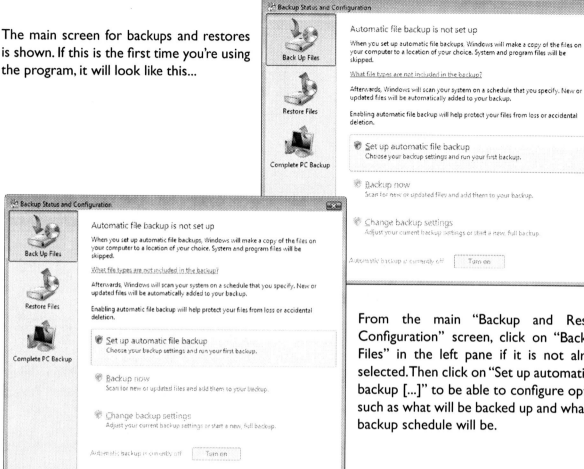

From the main "Backup and Restore Configuration" screen, click on "Back Up Files" in the left pane if it is not already selected. Then click on "Set up automatic file backup [...]" to be able to configure options such as what will be backed up and what the backup schedule will be.

If prompted, click "Continue" to open the backup configuration screen...

On the next screen, you'll select where you would like your backups to be saved. In my example, I'll be backing up files to my external USB hard drive that is already set up and turned on. My external hard drive has a drive letter of "G" - yours may be something different. If you are backing up to another computer on your network, you would select the "On a network" option. Once you've selected the correct location, click "Next."

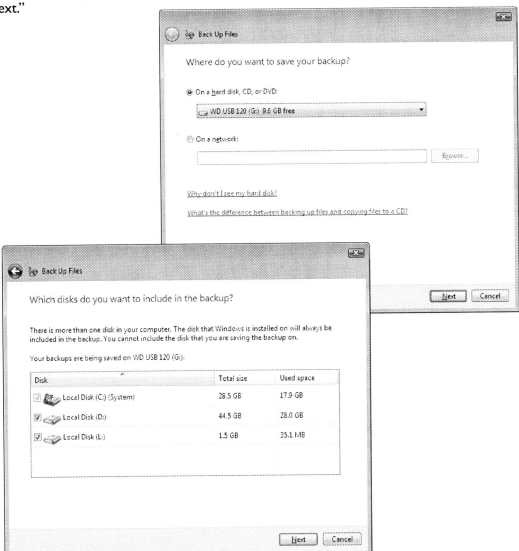

On the next screen, you'll choose the drives you want to back up. In my case, I have three partitions on my computer - I would like to back up files from each of the drives, so I ensured that all of them have been checked.

You are now shown a screen where you can select the types of files to be backed up. If possible, I would leave the default option of having all checkboxes selected. This will help ensure that all critical data files are backed up. Keep in mind that this type of backup does not back up your system files (like Windows), executables, or temporary files. The idea behind this type of backup is simply to ensure that your data itself (spreadsheets, documents, music files, digital pictures, etc.) is safely backed up in case you ever need to restore it. Click "Next" when you are ready to continue.

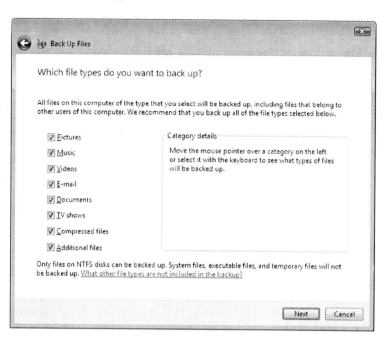

You now have the option to set a schedule as to how often you would like the backup to run. You can have the backups run daily, weekly, or monthly. Select the appropriate option and then choose the actual day and time to run. The backup will perform a full backup, backing up all selected files, and then only new and changed files on subsequent backups. Because of that, I would recommend running your backups on a frequent schedule if possible. Running your backups daily, for instance, will help ensure that if you need to restore files at a later point in time, you will be current up to within a day. If you run your backups once a month however, a restore could end up

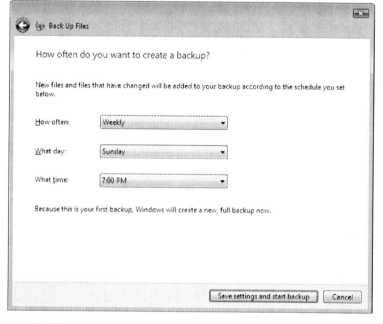

costing you a month's worth of files because your backup hasn't run for almost a month. I would also recommend running the backups at a time when you will not be using the computer (such as late at night or early in the morning), so that you're computer is not slowed down while the backup process is doing its thing. Once you've selected what makes sense for you, then click the "Save settings and start backup" button.

Your settings have now been saved and your first backup will begin. If you are prompted to insert the media, as long as the media is in place (external drive or DVD), click "OK."

The backup will then create a shadow copy to ensure that files being backed up are not in use when trying to be backed up and then the files will be backed up.

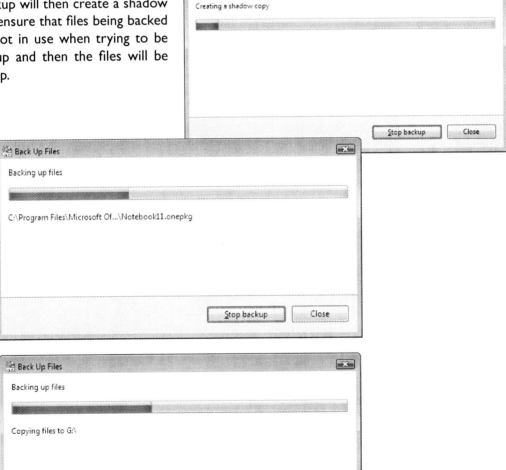

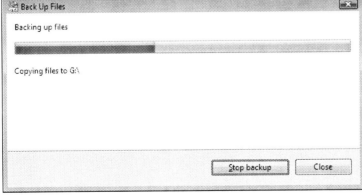

You will be notified when the backup completes...

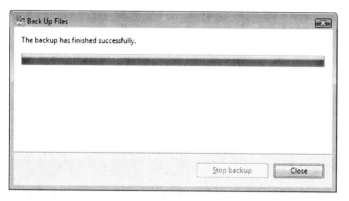

Keep in mind that for your scheduled backups to complete successfully, the computer and destination (such as an external hard drive) must be turned on.

If you ever need to change your settings, just go back into the backup utility and select the option to "Change backup settings" and follow the wizard.

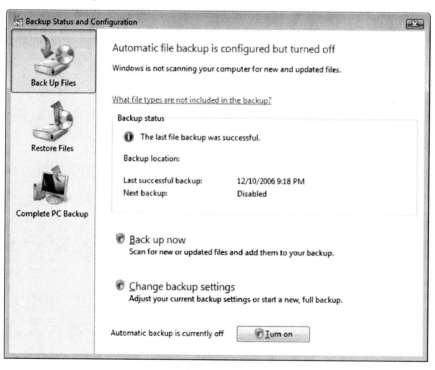

That's all there is to it. You can now take a little bit of a sigh of relief knowing that your data will be safely backed up on a regular basis.

chapter 23

Checking Your Backups

<u>Verifying backups / Test restores</u>

So you've convinced yourself that you need to start doing backups - you're set, right? Unfortunately, the answer is no. Backups can give you a false sense of security. I've worked with customers who had been doing their backups every day as part of their daily routine. Unfortunately, part of their routine was not to check the backups by performing test restores and they later found out that their data was not actually being backed up. They had plenty of tapes they labeled and put aside in case of emergency, but when the time actually came around, we came to find out the tapes were blank. Not something anyone would want to tell a customer, much less being the customer and having to hear that.

It is imperative that you are not only running backups, but that you verify in the backup software that the data was backed up successfully. Regardless of what the backup software reports, you should also periodically perform a test restore to make sure that the data is actually good on the DVD, USB drive, or whatever you're using. When I say periodically, I'm talking about asking yourself how far back you can afford to lose data. If you can lose a week's worth of data and not be too upset, then checking every week might be sufficient. If losing a couple days worth of data is not acceptable, then you need to be performing backups at least daily and trying a test restore daily as well.

Doing a test restore does not only mean looking on the media and making sure that you can see the files you need. You need to take a few of those files and copy or restore them to a folder on your computer and then actually try to open them and make sure they aren't corrupt. This is the ONLY way to be 100% sure your backed up data is good. I wouldn't recommend doing the test restore on every file - I'm sure you have better things to do. However, I would recommend that you test a few different files every time you do this, along with any files that are critical and can't afford to be lost.

The first thing that you'll want to do between backups is check the backup status or log files to ensure that the backup ran successfully...

Checking the backup status when using Windows Vista backup

In the Windows Vista OS, you can simply open up the "Backup Status and Configuration" program. Click on the appropriate type of backup you performed on the left ("Back Up Files" or "Complete PC Backup") and the status of the last backup will be shown.

For other backup software, you will want to review the software's documentation on how to check the log files.

If there are any problems flagged by the status or log files, you'll want to investigate the problem. If the error isn't self-explanatory, go to your favorite search engine like Google search (**http://www.google.com**) or the Yahoo! search engine (**http://www.yahoo.com**) and type in the error to learn more of what the error means and possible ways to correct the problem. And here's a tip... in many search engines (like Google or Yahoo!), by putting enclosing quotation marks the words you're searching for, the search engine will search for the phrase as a whole rather than individual words. This can be extremely helpful in narrowing down and pinpointing the exact error you're looking for.

Assuming that any backup errors have been corrected and your backups are running smoothly, you will now want to perform test restores on the data. To see how to do this when backing up your data using the "Back Up Files" program, refer to "Chapter 31 - Restoring Data with Windows Backup."

In summary, don't just run your backups and stop there. You can't reliably count on a truly successful backup without managing them as well. It is critical to both check the status of the backups (or log files) and to perform periodic restores of some or all of your data.

chapter 24

System Restore Points

There is one last thing I want to briefly go over before we move onto the next section. Starting with the Windows XP operating system and later improved upon in the Windows Vista OS is a feature called System Restore. In works like this... on regular intervals, the Windows OS will take a snapshot of your computer, which Microsoft refers to as "system restore points." The restore points are also created when certain applications or drivers are installed. They can also be created manually if desired by clicking on the "Start" button and then clicking on "Programs" or "All Programs," then "Accessories," "System Tools," and finally "System Restore." Then simply follow the prompts to create the restore point.

The idea is that the restore points are quick, point-in-time snapshots of your computer. You may not even know that they are being created. Even though restore points are for the most part transparent to users, they are one of the coolest things to be added into Windows.

Here's why... let's say that you find a new photo-editing software package that you want to try out. You install it on your computer and it prompts you to restart. You restart your computer and halfway through the Windows operating system startup, you get the infamous Blue Screen of Death - a bright blue screen telling you that Windows can't start. You restart the computer and you get the same thing. Now what do you do - start to do a restore of your last backup? What a hassle! Well, with the System Restore you can simply "roll back" your computer to the way it was before the software was installed. And, it probably won't even take you fifteen minutes to do!

To see the System Restore settings in the Windows Vista OS, click on the "Start" button, and in the search box, type in **sysdm.cpl** and then press the "Enter" key.

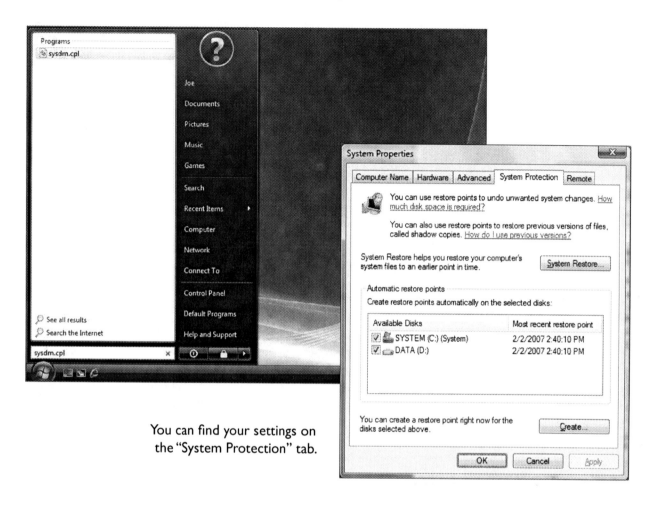

You can find your settings on
the "System Protection" tab.

I would recommend checking the box next to any drives that are not checked. This will help make restore points that can be used to restore previous versions of documents.

We'll get more into how to do the System Restore in the section on disaster recovery, but I wanted to let you know that the Windows operating system does do some important backup functionality of its own while you're working. It uses up to 15% of the space on each hard drive to store the restore points and automatically deletes the older restore points so it doesn't use up more than the set percentage of space. So, if you happen to come across the settings for System Restore, don't shut it off to save on drive space. Being able to quickly roll back to the way the Windows OS was in a previous state has saved me and many other people I know a lot of time and energy.

IX. The Basics of Disaster Recovery

chapter 25

Everyday Example

You've been making your regular backups and now the day of reckoning has come... your hard drive just crashed. You're in disbelief for a second, but you stay calm. You call technical support from the vendor who makes your computer (HP, Dell, etc.) and fill them in on what's going on. They tell you that the problem is that your hard drive crashed, but lucky for you, your computer is under warranty so they'll get another one shipped out to you immediately.

Great... glad that's taken care of. Oh, yeah - but wait a minute. That means you're going to have to get all your data back on your computer. If you've been taking care to routinely back up your data and test the backups to make sure that they've been successful, then this recovery process probably won't be too horrible for you!

This is an extremely plausible scenario. Hard drives are far from being full proof from becoming defective, and unfortunately, unless you've been following the advice of the previous section, you've been keeping all your eggs in one basket. If that's the case, you now may need to throw your hands up in the air and start from scratch.

Let's hold that thought on the crashed hard drive. Let's start with something a little simpler and then we'll come back to that example a little bit later.

So let's say that a non-hardware problem occurs on your computer - something within Windows that causes dramatic problems. Here are some examples of what I'm talking about:

- A virus gets on your computer and starts changing or deleting system files causing the Windows OS to keep giving you errors.
- Some type of malware gets on your computer slowing it to a crawl, and no matter how hard you (or a computer guru you know) try to get rid of it, it keeps coming back.
- A new software application or an update to an existing application causes a conflict with some other program, and now the other program doesn't work.
- You install a new piece of hardware (such as a printer, scanner, USB drive, etc.) causing your computer to give you the "Blue Screen of Death," a notorious way the Windows operating system lets you know it has a problem that it can't get past.
- An update for the Windows OS gets released from Microsoft and after Windows installs it for you, Microsoft realizes that it causes problems and releases a press release telling users not to install it - a little too late.

Unbelievably, in many cases such as the ones above, you might be able to get back up and running quickly using Windows System Restore. As discussed in "Chapter 24 - System Restore Points," the Windows XP and Windows Vista operating systems automatically create periodic restore points. These can be used to restore the Windows OS to a point in time before a problem occurred.

The chapters in the rest of this section help guide you through trying to get up and running - starting with the simplest method and working through to a worst-case scenario.

chapter 26

Previous Versions / System Restore

Previous Versions

The Windows Vista operating system contains a feature called "Previous Versions" that uses the Microsoft "Volume Shadow Copy" technology. This was created originally in the Windows XP and Windows Server 2003 operating systems and provides some excellent file protection.

As long as "System Protection" is turned on for any hard drives on your computer (see "Chapter 24 - System Restore Points"), the Windows Vista OS will periodically create what it refers to as "Shadow Copies." These "Shadow Copies" are created from files that have been modified since the last restore point was created. This typically occurs about once a day.

The nice thing about this is the extra layer of protection you are given. Let's say that you are working on a Microsoft Word document you had created yesterday and today you make some changes to the document and save it. You then think about it and wish you hadn't have saved those changes. Before the Windows Vista operating system, there was not much you could about this scenario unless you would go through the hassle of performing a restore from a backup that was made last night... assuming a backup was even created last night.

Now, however, you can just right-click on the document and choose "Restore previous versions" (as long as "System Protection" is turned on for the partition where the file is located). This will list any previous versions of the file that the Windows Vista OS has created.

You can then click on a particular version, open it to see what it is, copy it to a different location, or restore it over the current document.

Keep in mind that if you choose "Restore," you will be overwriting the file that is currently out there. When prompted, be sure to only click "Restore" if you're certain that's what you want to do.

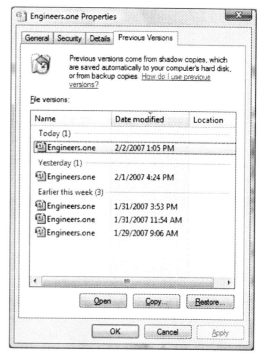

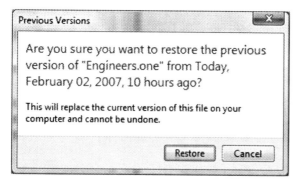

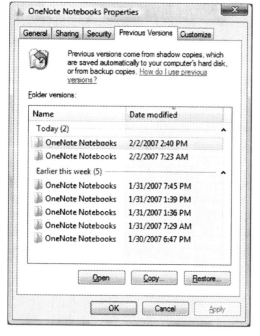

Now, if you had deleted the file and wanted to restore it, obviously you can't right-click on the file and choose "Restore previous versions" because the file isn't there to do that. All you need to do in that case is right-click on the folder that contained the file (or the drive if it was in the root of the drive), right-click on it, and choose "Restore previous versions." The only difference is that you now see the folder listed instead of the file.

Unless you want the entire folder restored, I would select the instance you want to get back, choose "Open," and then browse to the file you want to restore in the window that comes up. Keep in mind that the window that comes up is actually what is stored in the "Shadow Copy." Once you find the file you want, right-click on it and select "Copy." You can then go to the actual location on your hard drive where you want to restore it to (like your Desktop), right-click in an empty place of the window, and choose "Paste."

"Previous Versions" is an excellent way to take care of files that you may have mistakenly modified or if you deleted a file and then emptied it out of the "Recycle Bin." Always remember this as a first line of defense before continuing with some of the more drastic matters in the upcoming chapters because it's quick and simple.

Normal Mode System Restore

The power of the System Restore can help you recover your computer from a Windows operating system or software problem quickly and generally quite effectively. Microsoft first added the System Restore feature in the Windows XP OS. Here's how to use the functionality to perform a restore in Windows Vista OS.

If the problem hasn't rendered Windows useless and you can work your way around from within Windows, click on the "Start" button, go to "Programs" or "All Programs," then "Accessories," "System Tools," and select "System Restore." If prompted for permission, click "Continue" or enter in the password for an administrator account.

 or

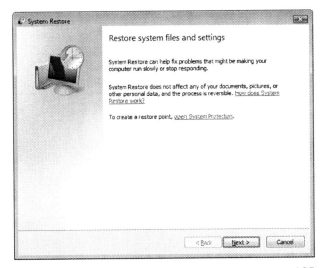

You can then click "Next" to get started...

Please keep in mind that right before the restore is performed, another restore point is automatically created. That way if the restore does not work, you can run this again and go back to the point you are at now. Another important note is that the restore only affects the Windows operating system files - it does not affect your personal files (documents, digital photos, email, etc.). This is NOT meant to be a way to restore deleted files. If that is what you are trying to do, you should be doing a restore from a backup instead.

You will now be presented with a list of the available restore points. Try to pick the one that goes back just far

enough without going back too far or it may affect software that was installed or updated since that time (in which case you may need to reinstall the software). Thankfully, many of the restore points are created by the installation of software programs right before the software is installed. So if you have a major problem on your computer, you can usually restore to the moment before the installation occurred. Select the restore point you would like to restore and click "Next."

You are now presented with a confirmation screen. You will want to make sure all programs are closed before continuing. Click "Finish" and you will prompted one more time with the "Are you sure" type of warning... click "Yes" to continue and the restore process will begin. Your computer will automatically be restarted during this process.

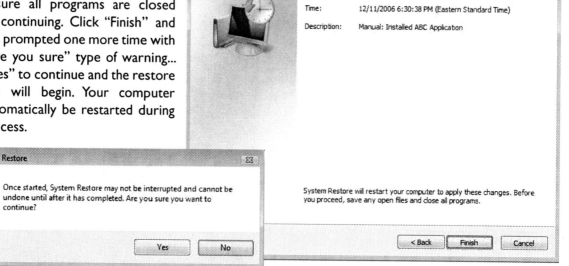

The system restore process will then begin...

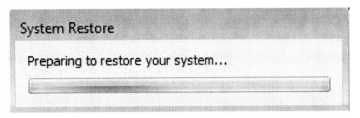

After a little while (a few minutes on my test run), your computer should automatically restart and bring you back to the login screen. Once you log in, you'll then get one more prompt to tell you that the restore was successful (or to alert you of any problems).

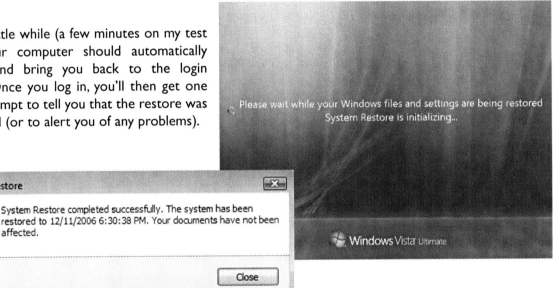

Click "Close" and you should be taken back to your desktop. Now comes the true test - if your problems went away, great... you're done. If the problem did not go away, you may want to try repeating the process choosing an earlier restore point. If for some reason, a whole slew of problems arose because of this restore and you just want to go back to the way it was, you'll want to repeat the process choosing the restore point that was created right before the restore was performed (a sort of "undo" feature).

Safe Mode System Restore

If you can't boot successfully into the Windows operating system, you can try starting the process from "Safe Mode." "Safe Mode" is a method of starting that the Windows OS uses where it only allows the necessary files and drivers to load to get the Windows operating system running. In many cases, that means that if you have something causing problems in the Windows OS, "Safe Mode" doesn't allow that to load and you can get in and make changes that would otherwise be difficult or impossible to do. It may also be another way for you to get into the Windows OS to do a System Restore.

To get into "Safe Mode," restart your computer. As the computer is starting up, but before Windows launches, press F8 several times until you see a menu of different options. If you see the black screen with only the Windows Vista OS progress bar, you missed it. Restart your computer and try again. Once you do get to the menu of options, use the arrow keys to select "Safe Mode" and hit "Enter." You may need to select the operating system to start... in most cases, there will be only one for the Windows Vista OS.

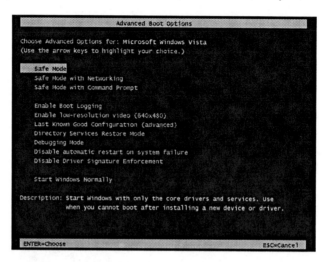

When the Windows operating system finishes loading, you will probably need to choose whom you want to log in as. I would recommend first trying to log in as a user with Administrator privileges to ensure that adequate permissions are there for the restore. As a side note, the first user created in Windows Vista during installation is part of the Administrators group.

Once logged in, you will simply, click on the "Start" button, go to "Programs" or "All Programs," then "Accessories," "System Tools," and select "System Restore." This will launch the System Restore program. Then just follow the same instructions from the beginning of the chapter.

System Restore from the Windows OS DVD

To give you another option, if you can't boot successfully into the Windows OS normally or through "Safe Mode," you can use your Windows Vista operating system DVD. The only problem with this is that some computer vendors may not include the full Windows Vista DVD with the computer when you purchase it.

However, if you do have the DVD, you can place it in the DVD tray and then restart the computer. When you see the message "Press any key to boot from CD or DVD...," press the spacebar or another key to allow the files from the Windows Vista DVD to load.

Once the necessary Windows operating system files are loaded, you will be presented with an "Install Windows" screen. Ensure that the correct language and other options are correct and then click "Next."

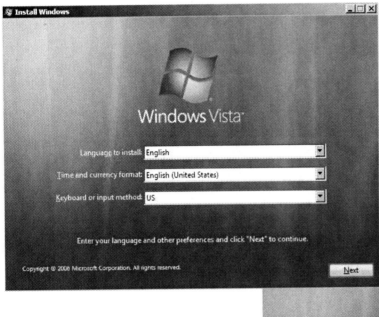

At this next "Install Windows" screen, select the hyperlink in the bottom left that says "Repair your computer"...

The DVD will then search for existing installations of the Windows Vista OS on your computer. If your installation does not show up in the list, you will not be able to continue. It is likely that your installation is highly corrupt beyond the basics. You can continue to try other options in this section, but you will probably need to do an entire restore to get back up and running (this is discussed later in this section). Otherwise, ensure that your Windows Vista installation is selected and then click "Next."

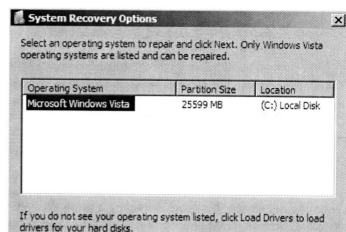

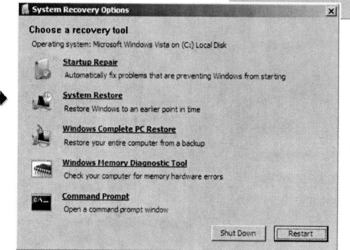

When the "System Recovery Options" dialog box appears, you will want to select "System Restore."

This will take you to the System Restore wizard. Select "Next" and then just continue to follow the instructions from the beginning of the chapter.

With any luck, now that you've gone through this chapter, your computer is alive and well. If not, the Windows Vista OS offers us a couple other recovery options...

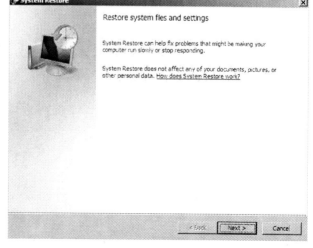

chapter 27

Startup Repair

If the Windows Vista OS won't start for you, an option you will probably want to try is the new "Startup Repair" feature. This feature will do its best to examine many of the most common Windows startup problems. If it is able to successfully diagnose the problem, it will also try to fix it. Keep in mind that this is generally run automatically if the Windows Vista operating system detects a problem itself trying to load. However, this may still be an option you may want to try if you're getting desperate.

As with some of the other troubleshooting tools, you need to use your Windows Vista operating system DVD. If your computer vendor did not include the full Windows Vista DVD with the computer (some don't), then you won't be able to do this.

If you do have the DVD, you can place it in the DVD tray and then restart the computer. When you see the message "Press any key to boot from CD or DVD...," press the spacebar or another key to allow the files from the Windows Vista DVD to load.

Once the necessary Windows files are loaded, you will be presented with an "Install Windows" screen. Ensure that the correct language and other options are correct and then click "Next."

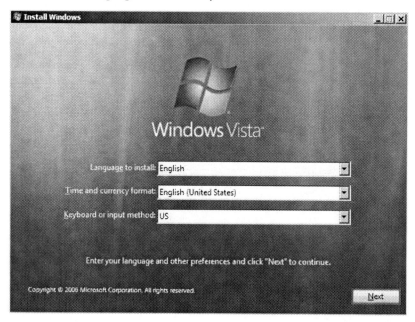

At the next "Install Windows" screen, select the hyperlink in the bottom left that says "Repair your computer"...

The DVD will then search for existing installations of the Windows Vista OS on your computer. If your installation does not show up in the list, you will not be able to continue. If that is the case, it is likely that your installation is highly corrupt beyond the basics. You can continue to try other options in this section, but you will probably need to be doing an entire restore to get back up and running (this is discussed later in this section). Otherwise, ensure that your Windows Vista installation is selected and then click "Next."

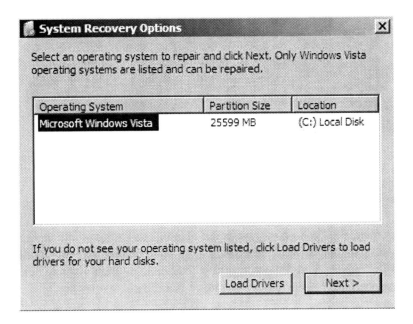

When the "System Recovery Options" dialog box comes up, you will want to select "Startup Repair."

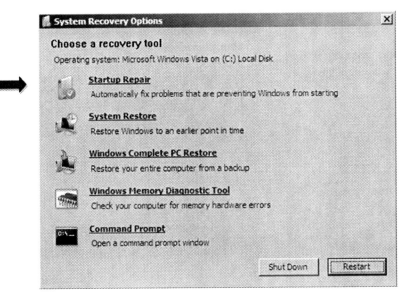

The tool will then begin to attempt the diagnosis and repair of your Windows OS startup problem...

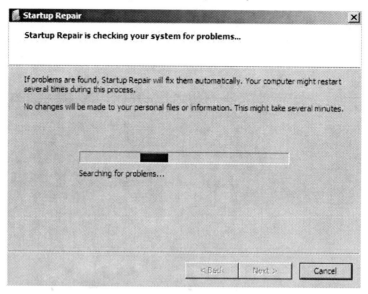

Just let the tool do its thing. If it finds a problem, it will attempt to fix it, and it may restart your computer several times during this process, so don't be alarmed. If it does restart, you will see the "Press any key to boot from CD or DVD..." message each time. You do NOT want to press any key during this process. The Windows operating system will handle going into the right mode as necessary.

After the Windows OS has been repaired, you will then be alerted that the repair is complete and you will have the ability to see the details of the repairs and logging.

If no problem is found during the process, you should get a dialog box similar to the following:

I hope that this helped you out. If not, then you might want to try a Complete PC restore...

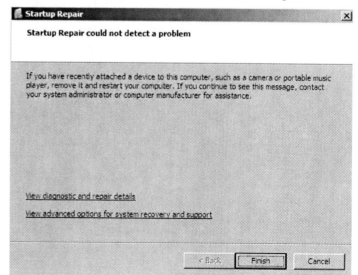

chapter 28

Complete PC Restore

If you're now reading this chapter in desperation, then you're probably having some major problems with your computer. Please make sure that you've read the previous chapters of this section first, because when you continue with this chapter, you're likely going to lose at least some data.

The Windows Vista OS introduced a new type of backup functionality called Complete PC backups. Complete PC backups create a point-in-time image of your computer as discussed in the section on backups. The only way that this chapter will benefit you at all is if you have previously created a Complete PC backup. If you've done at least one of these backups then you're ready to go!

Just keep in mind that the restoration of the image will put your computer exactly the way it was when the image was created. This means that any files or applications that have been created, modified, or deleted on the partition to be restored since the time of the Complete PC backup will be undone. This is something extremely important that you will want to consider before continuing. If you haven't done a Complete PC backup in quite some time, this can be a huge deal. If you perform regular data backups, you can later reinstall any applications since the Complete PC backup and then restore data from your regular backups. If not, then you may want to work with an experienced computer professional to help you get any critical data off the computer before continuing.

Once you're ready to go, make sure that the location of the Complete PC backups is connected and accessible. For example, if the backups you created are on an external hard drive, the hard drive should be connected and turned on so it can be located by Windows Vista for use in the restore process. You need to use the Windows Vista operating system DVD to boot into the Windows Recovery Environment. Put the DVD in the DVD tray and then restart the computer. When you see the message "Press any key to boot from CD or DVD...," press the spacebar or another key to allow the files from the Windows Vista DVD to load.

Once the necessary Windows operating system files are loaded, you will be presented with an "Install Windows" screen. Ensure that the correct language and other options are correct and then click "Next."

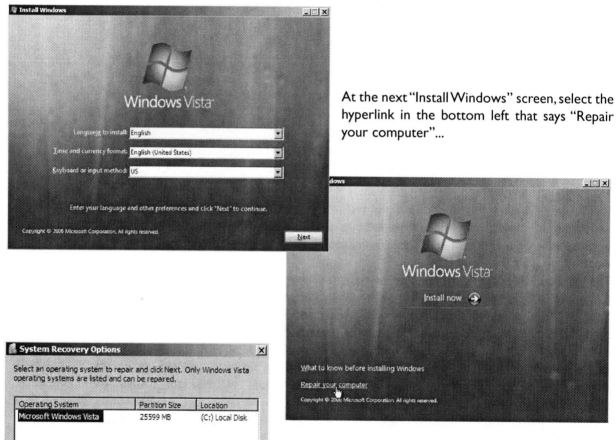

At the next "Install Windows" screen, select the hyperlink in the bottom left that says "Repair your computer"...

The DVD will then search for existing installations of the Windows Vista OS on your computer. Ensure that your Windows Vista installation is selected and then click "Next."

196

When the "System Recovery Options" dialog box comes up, you will want to select "Windows Complete PC Restore."

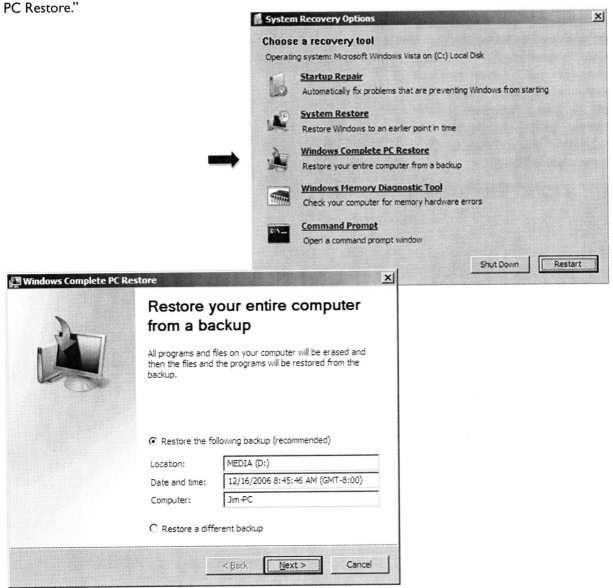

The "Windows Complete PC Restore" wizard will then start. The backup should find the last Complete PC backup and set that as the recommended backup to use for the restore. If you need to select a different one, then check the "Restore a different backup" option. Otherwise, leave the default as is and click "Next."

You will then be shown a confirmation of the backup to be restored. You also will see an option to "Format and repartition disks." This will make sure that your hard drive partitions (the "C" drive and in some cases "D" and maybe others) are deleted, recreated, and formatted to be the same size as they were at the time of the backup. If this option is not available, it will be grayed out. In the example you see here, I'm restoring from the "D" drive, so it obviously can't delete it. Once you're ready, click "Finish." You will be given a "just making sure" prompt and upon checking the "I confirm" box and clicking "OK," the restore will begin.

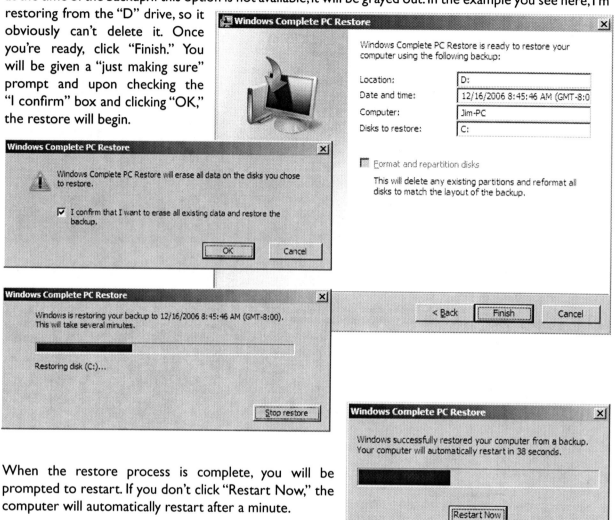

When the restore process is complete, you will be prompted to restart. If you don't click "Restart Now," the computer will automatically restart after a minute.

After the restart, you can log in to the computer as normal. You'll want to verify that everything is now working correctly, and you will need to reinstall any software applications that had been installed since you had made the Complete PC backup. You will also want to go to the Microsoft Update site and ensure that you have all updates that were released after you had made the Complete PC backup. Finally, if you've made regular "non-Complete PC" backups, you will probably want to restore any data files that are missing. Restoring files will be discussed later in this section.

chapter 29

System Restore Disks

Well, you've tried the methods in the previous chapters to try to get Windows Vista operating system up and running and still need some help. This chapter may help you out. With most major computer vendors, when you purchase a new computer, they give you a bunch of CDs/DVDs. If you're lucky, one or more of those CDs/DVDs are "System Restore" disks. It's important to know that this is different from the Windows Vista built-in System Restore functionality.

In a nutshell, the System Restore disks will put your computer *exactly* the way it was when you first installed it. That means *everything* - Windows, applications, system drivers, etc. Keep in mind that generally when you use the restore disks, it works by dropping all partitions on the computer and then putting the original computer image back on. So be careful when using this option because any applications, data, hardware drivers, etc. will be gone when using this. Essentially, you'll be starting from scratch. However, it will also usually get you up and running in a small amount of time (maybe a half-hour or so).

Every computer manufacturer is different in how their "System Restore" works, so there's no way I can hit on each method here. However, most work either by putting the restore CD/DVD into the drive and restarting the computer or by pressing a certain key when turning on your computer (before the Windows operating system starts).

Some vendors don't provide System Restore disks - they may provide a partition on your hard drive (visible or hidden) with the image on it. You'll need to check with your computer manufacturer to know how yours is set up.

To help point you in the right direction, there is an excellent resource called Windows Reinstall, a website run by Mark Walmsley for a number of years now. It is found at **http://www.windowsreinstall.com**. There is a section on their site (currently located at **http://oem.windowsreinstall.com**) specifically dedicated to providing resources about restoring computers from different manufacturers that should help get you started.

If you do decide to go with this approach, you'll want to make sure you've backed up anything that might be critical to you if possible. I hope that you've already been following the section of this book on backups and have everything already backed up. If not, you may want to return to that section and try to back up anything important to you so you can restore it back to your computer once you've used the System Restore disks.

chapter 30

Format then Reinstall the Windows Vista OS

Whether you've run into problems that have made your computer a pain to work with or you've simply noticed that over time your computer has begun to run a lot slower than when you first started using it, it might be time to do a fresh install of the Windows operating system. This is not a quick task and will take you some time to get it back to the way you want it, but the good news is that starting from scratch clears up all of your problems!

Here's what needs to be done...
1. First, you need to make sure that you back up anything that you want to keep, including data and personal settings.
2. Find and download a couple of critical drivers for Windows Vista.
3. You'll then reformat the Windows OS partition and install a fresh copy of the Windows Vista operating system.
4. After installing the Windows Vista OS, you need to make sure all updates are installed.
5. Next, you'll need to reinstall any software applications, including virus protection and apply any necessary patches to get the software current.
6. Finally, you'll restore any data or settings that you need back.

Now keep in mind that similar to what you've read in some of the previous chapters, you will need the full operating system DVD for the Windows Vista OS. If you do not have this, you won't be able to perform the Windows Vista installation, unless you have something like the computer's "System Restore" disks as discussed previously. You should also make sure that if your Windows Vista DVD requires a product key, that you have it handy because you will need it during installation. The product key is usually five sets of a combination of five letters or numbers each (a total of 25 characters long).

So, let's get started...

The first thing that you need to do is back up any necessary data and personal settings. If you haven't read the "The Basics of Backups" section, then you should definitely stop right now, read over what should be backed up and how to perform the backup, and then come back to this chapter.

It is important that the backup of your data and settings is made to a location that is not stored on the same partition as the Windows operating system (usually the C drive) because when we do our format and reinstall of the Windows OS, anything on that partition will be gone. Your best bet is to back up the data to a location outside of your computer, such as an external hard drive. Follow the section on backups to see how to perform the backup if you're unsure.

Once your backup has been completed, be sure to perform a test restore of some of your most important files as discussed in "Chapter 23 - Checking Your Backups." This is critical - remember that we are dropping everything that is on your computer, so if the backup turns out to be bad, that data is likely gone!

Now, I'm going to pass on something that's been a "gotcha" for me before. The Windows Vista operating system is very good at identifying and installing the necessary drivers for devices on computers. However, it doesn't know all of them. Moreover, if it can't find the right driver for a device, then that device can't be used in the Windows operating system. Most device manufacturers will let you download the latest driver from their website. My "gotcha" turned out to be that I hadn't downloaded some important drivers before installing the Windows XP OS years ago and when it was done, it couldn't identify my network card. No network card equals no Internet connection. No Internet connection means I can't download the driver for the network card. How's that for funny?

I eventually downloaded the driver from another computer and then burned it to a CD to get it to my computer, but the point is it was a real pain. The moral of the story is you can download any drivers you might be missing after the installation of the Windows operating system is complete. However, I would highly recommend downloading drivers for your network card if that's your connection to the Internet. If you're still using dial-up to the Internet, then you want to make sure you download the drivers for your modem.

Many vendors provide CDs that contain the drivers for all hardware that came with your computer. If not, then you will want to try going to the computer manufacturer's website to see if you can download the drivers from there. For example on HP or Dell's websites, you can go to the support page, put in your computer model and version of Windows, and then download the necessary drivers from there. Again, I highly recommend that you do this before continuing and then either include them as part of your backup or copy them off your computer to use later.

All right, onto the fun part... don't get nervous - this won't be too bad! To show you how to perform this, I will be using Windows Vista Ultimate Edition. If you have a different version of the Windows Vista operating system, don't worry - the instructions and screenshots for installation will be almost identical.

Put the Windows Vista operating system DVD into the DVD tray and then restart the computer. When you see the message "Press any key to boot from CD or DVD...," press the spacebar or another key to allow the files from the Windows Vista DVD to load. Be patient while the Windows DVD loads necessary setup files...

The next screen will be the "Install Windows" screen. Adjust the installation settings if necessary and then click "Next."

On this next screen, simply select "Install now."

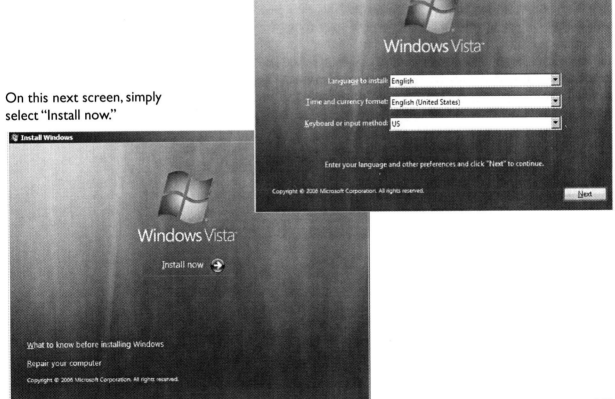

When the screen comes up to "Get important updates for installation," I would recommend selecting the first option to "Go online to get the latest updates for installation (recommended) [...]."

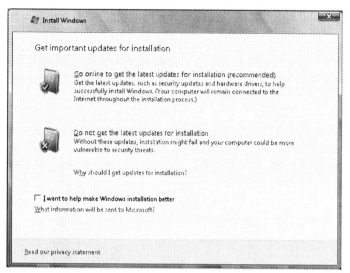

You will then likely be prompted for your product key. I'm hoping you put that aside before your started the installation as I mentioned at the beginning of the chapter! You'll also probably see a checkbox to "Automatically activate Windows when I'm online." What that means is that the Windows OS will need to be registered with Microsoft over the Internet to allow you to use the computer. This is done as to stop people from taking their copy of the Windows operating system and installing it on other peoples' computers (usually referred to as piracy or in its very essence... stealing). By activating, an algorithm based off certain specifications of your computer is sent to Microsoft. The idea is that your copy of the Windows operating system is then tied to that computer. There is some flexibility in this activation to help take into consideration if you upgrade different parts of your computer or if you get a new computer altogether.

You can either let the Windows OS do the activation for you automatically once it detects a connection to the Internet by checking the box or you can manually perform activation once the Windows OS is installed. I would recommend waiting until it is installed so you can ensure everything is working properly before you activate it. Once you've put in your product key and selected if you want activation to occur automatically, click "Next."

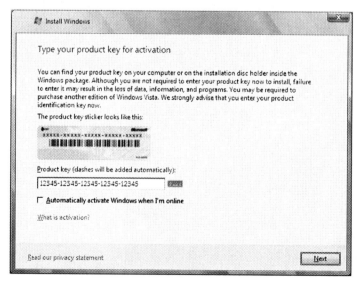

The next screen will be to accept the license agreement. Feel free to read the whole agreement if you want, but in order to continue, you must check the box to say you accept the agreement in order to enable the "Next" button.

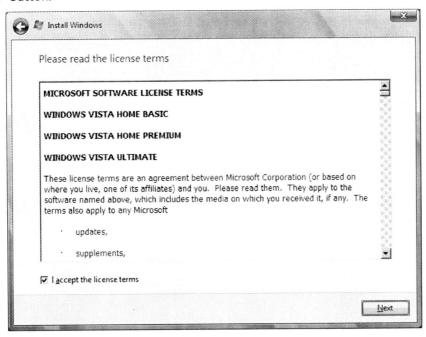

You're now presented with the installation type screen. Because you've booted right from the CD, your only option is to click "Custom (advanced)."

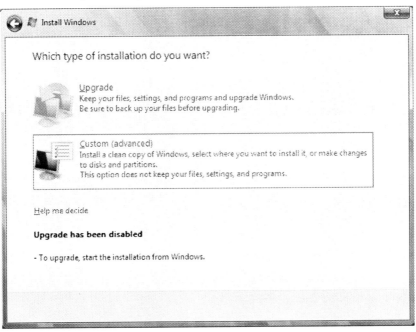

On the "Where do you want to install Windows?" screen, you're shown a list of the partitions on your computer. Remember that partitions are just logical breakups of a hard drive. Therefore, even though you may only have only one physical hard drive, you may have more than one logical "drive" on your computer. Those "drives" are likely to actually be partitions on the hard drive. In the screenshot, you'll see that there are two partitions on the hard drive. To be able to delete the Windows operating system partition, you'll first need to click on that partition and then click "Drive options (advanced)" to give us some more options.

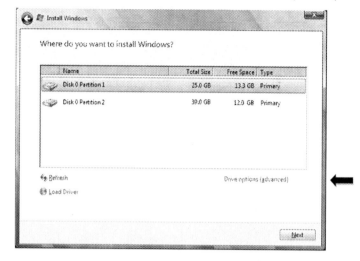

Here comes the moment of truth - we now want to delete the Windows operating system partition. In most cases, for the typical PC user, "Disk 0 Partition 1" will be your Windows installation. An exception might be if the computer manufacturer has a small utility partition on the drive, for example. Make sure that you have the Windows partition selected and then select "Delete."

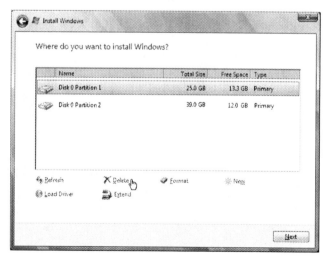
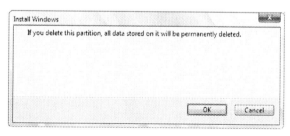

Setup will now let you know that deleting the partition will destroy all data on it. As long as you know that you have a good backup of your data, click "OK."

Since we deleted the partition, it now becomes unallocated space.

You may have had more than one partition on your hard drive. You do not need to delete any other partitions you may have - they may contain data on them that you want. You may also see a partition on your computer that might be a recovery partition for your computer. This could be used to restore your computer back to factory defaults. It's up to you what to do with any of the partitions. If you are sure what each partition is and want to delete them, you can repeat the steps we just went through for deleting the Windows operating system partition. If you are not sure what the partition is, you may not want to delete it at this time.

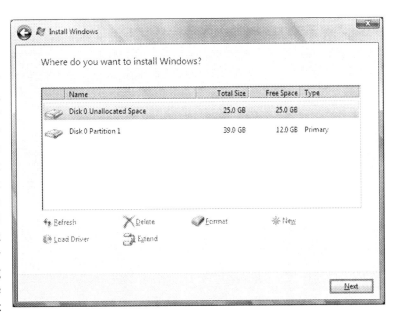

If desired, you could now create different partitions on your hard drive, such as a partition for the Windows operating system and a partition for your data. Keep in mind that you probably want to leave a _minimum_ of 15 GB (15,360 MB) for the Windows OS. I would recommend making it 20 GB (20,480 MB) or 25 GB (25,600 MB) as long as you have the space. To create partitions, you can select "New" and set up the correct sizes.

When creating partitions, you can select "Format" to set up the file structure that will be used. You will see some different options here for FAT and NTFS. FAT is an older type of file system that was used in the MS-DOS® operating system (FAT16) and then introduced as FAT32 in the Windows 95 Service Pack 2 operating system. NTFS is a file system that started with the Windows NT OS and provides many advantages over FAT32, such as better security, fault tolerance, and encryption. It is the current file system used by Microsoft and preferred in almost every new Windows Vista OS installation.

So why does Microsoft even offer FAT as an option? The reason is that FAT is more universal and can be read by other operating systems (such as Linux or Mac OS), whereas NTFS generally cannot be. If you were going to have more than one operating system on your computer and wanted to be able to get to the data from whichever operating system you are in, you would probably want to use FAT. My recommendation is to use NTFS unless this situation applies to you. Microsoft states "NTFS is the recommended file system for Windows Vista" on a web page of theirs dealing with the Windows Vista OS. This and more information on file systems can currently be found at: **http://www.microsoft.com/ technet/windowsvista/library/plan/5025760b-0433-4ba1-a2f4-9338915fdb4b.mspx?mfr=true.**

In our example, we are just going to install onto the same size partition as the Windows operating system had before. We could select "New" to create the partition, but if the unallocated space is the size you would like the Windows installation to be, just highlight it, and then select "Next." Windows setup will save us a couple steps, automatically creating the partition for us and formatting it as NTFS.

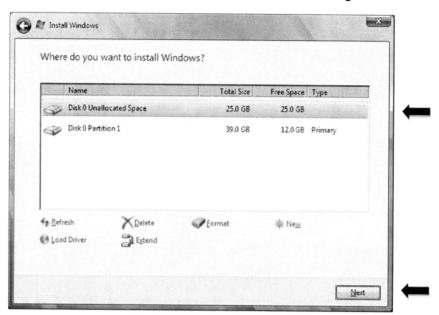

Setup will then jump right into copying files and installing the Windows Vista operating system. You might as well get a couple cups of coffee for this one! No user interaction will be required until the end. Here's a little bit of the walk through to show you some of what you'll see during the installation...

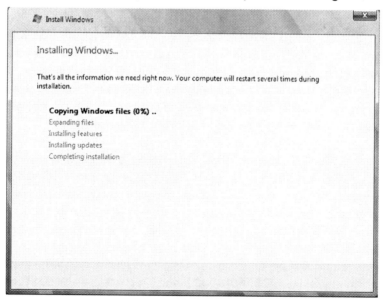

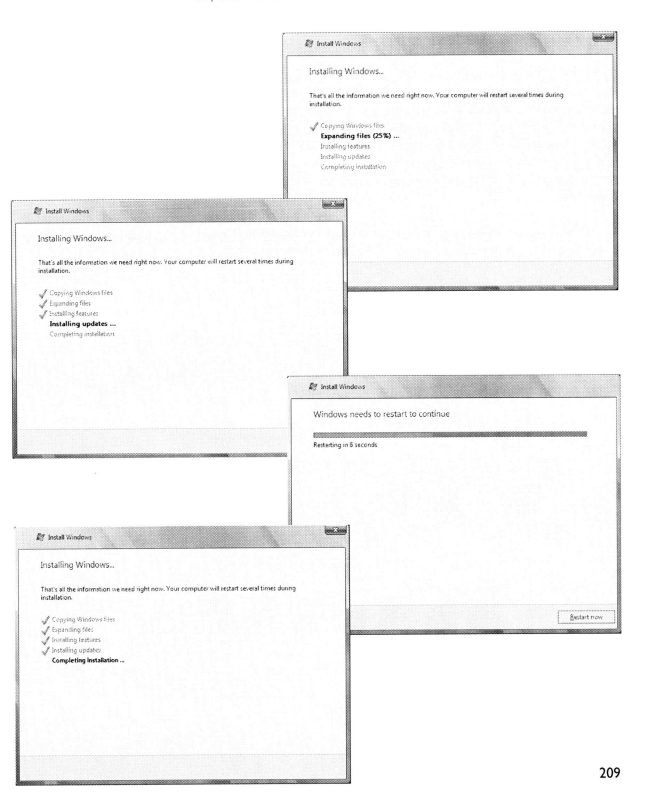

Welcome back! It's time to do a little personalization...

On the "Choose a user name and picture" screen, you can put in your name. This will be the default account and will be set up as an administrator account on the computer. You also have an opportunity to set up a password. If this is a laptop computer, I would strongly recommend that you create a good, solid password. If this is your home computer, I would still recommend setting up a password, but that is up to you. Be careful if you fill in the box for a "password hint." This can be seen by anyone using the computer. So if you put in the password hint field "My middle name," then anyone who goes to log onto the computer can see that and if they know your middle name, they know your password. I would recommend not filling in this field.

You can also choose a picture to be associated with your account. This shows up on the Welcome screen as well as a couple other places, such as at the top of the programs menu.

Once you've filled in everything necessary, click "Next."

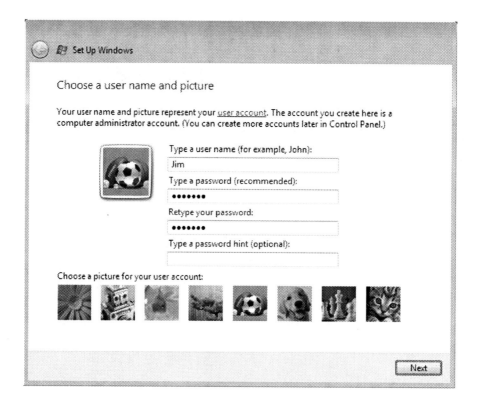

Setup will now give you the opportunity to name your computer. I'd recommend not making too revealing about who you are. You can see I decided to name this one "Jim-PC" - it doesn't have my last name or anything like that. Once you've named your computer, click "Next."

On the "Help protect Windows automatically" screen, you can decide if you'd like to get Windows up to date. Just as Microsoft is trying to emphasize here, I would recommend choosing "Use recommended settings." This will get your computer up to date with security fixes. It will also look for the latest computer drivers, and ensure the spyware protection (Windows Defender) is current.

Next, we need to set up the Windows Vista operating system with the current date, time, and time zone information. Make sure you take your time and enter things correctly here. Many things have become dependent on this information to be correct, particularly if you are networking with other equipment, such as a server. Once you've set this information, click "Next."

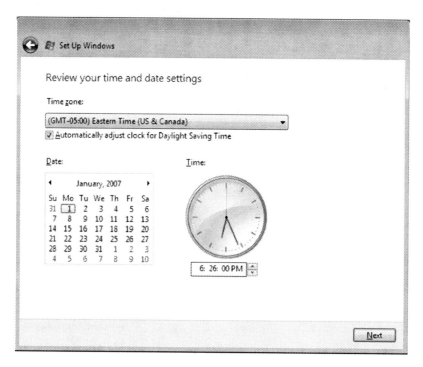

If the Windows operating system was able to establish a network connection, you'll get a prompt to choose a location where the computer will be used. The idea is that based on whether you choose "Home," "Work," or "Public location," Windows can then apply security settings that make the most sense for the environment.

For instance, if you select "Home," the Windows OS is a little less restrictive in its setup. It allows Network Discovery as well as file and printer sharing and opens up the appropriate ports on the Windows Firewall. This option is designed with the home or home office user in mind.

On the other hand, the option for "Public location" is designed for networks in public places such as a coffee shop. The idea is that you'll want to keep your computer more secure. To help with this, Network Discovery is shut off by default.

If you're not sure what to select (such as if it's a laptop that you will use at different places like home and in public places), then go with "Public location." The highest security settings will then be applied.

Choose the appropriate option and then choose "OK." Keep in mind that you can always switch categories by going into the "Control Panel," then clicking "Network and Internet," and finally clicking on "Network and Sharing Center."

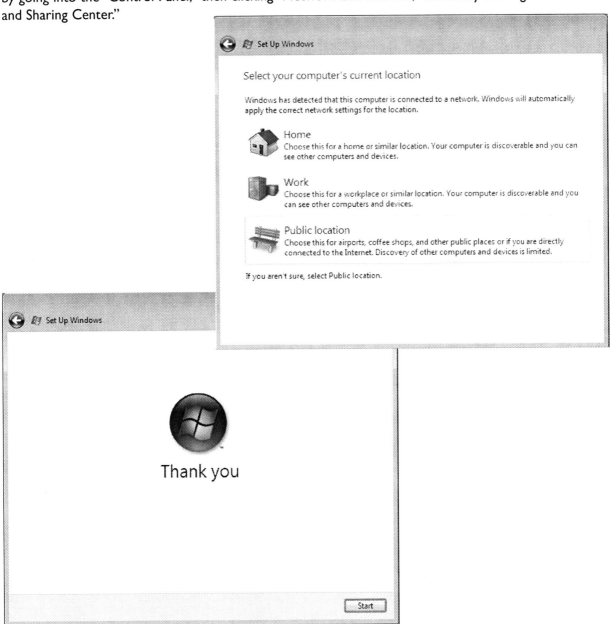

Congratulations! You've just installed the Windows Vista operating system. Click on "Start" to go to the Welcome screen.

You should now be taken to the login screen. Enter your password (if you created one) and click on the arrow next to the password to log in. If you did not set a password, click on the picture you set for your account to log in.

Once your user profile loads, the desktop will be displayed. Keep in mind that it may take a couple minutes to create everything for your new profile, so give it a little time.

The first thing you should do is ensure that all updates have been installed from Windows Update. In the Windows Vista OS, Windows Update is no longer a website. It is found by clicking on the "Start" button, clicking on "All Programs," and then going to "Windows Update." You can also get to it by going into the "Control Panel" and then clicking on "Check for updates" under the "Security" topic.

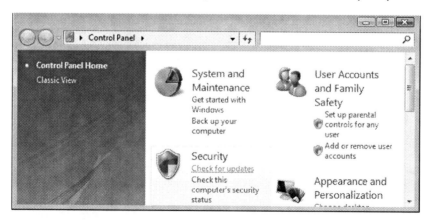

I would recommend installing all updates that are available for your computer. First click the "Check for updates" link and then after the check is complete, click the "Install updates" button.

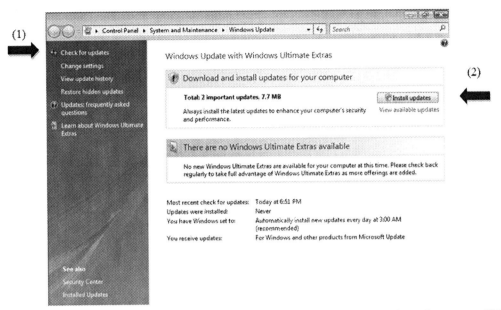

The next step is to install your anti-virus software (if you don't have any, go back to the section "The Basics of Protecting Your Computer," and be sure to get this!). Make sure to update the anti-virus software with the latest signature files to bring it up to date.

After that, you can start installing any of the applications that you need on computer as well as any updates that the applications need.

Once you've gotten your applications installed on your computer, you should be ready to bring back over your data. If you copied your data elsewhere, simply copy it back to the same location on your new installation. If you backed up your data using Windows Backup, continue onto the next chapter to see how to restore just what you need back onto your computer.

chapter 31

Restoring Data with Windows Backup

Earlier, you learned how to perform backups of important data on your computer. Now it's time to restore this data back onto your computer. If you used a third-party application to perform your backup, you'll have to figure out how to restore the data back yourself using that particular application and the help file if necessary. If, however, you used Windows Backup, then I can show you how to restore your data.

Now that you already know how to back up your data with Windows Backup, you'll see that restoring data back to your computer is just as easy.

Please note that you must be logged in with an administrator account in order to be able to perform an "Advanced restore" in the Windows Vista operating system, which is what I'm about to take you through.

The first thing you'll want to do is make sure that if you have your backups on an external hard drive, that it is connected and powered on. Then you'll need to launch Windows Backup. Click on the "Start" button, then go to "Programs" or "All Programs" (depending on how your "Start" menu is set up), then go to "Accessories," "System Tools," and then select "Backup Status and Configuration."

When the backup program opens, click on "Restore Files" in the left pane and then click on the "Advanced restore" button...

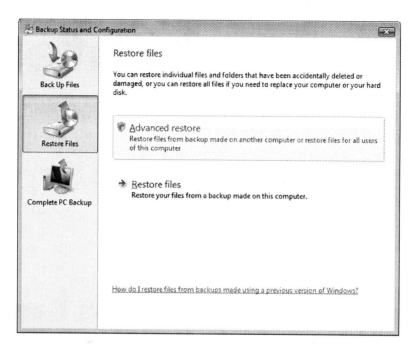

If prompted for permission, click "Continue."

When you get to the prompt asking you what you want to restore, I'm going to take you through with an assumption that you just went through the process of formatting and reinstalling the Windows Vista OS by means of one of the earlier chapters in this section. Even if you didn't, the following will still work for you.

Select the option for "Files from a backup made on a different computer." You might be thinking, "But this is not a different computer - I'm restoring to the same computer I backed up the data from!" That's true, but your computer doesn't know that you've just rebuilt your computer through a formatting and reinstallation process. If you select one of the other options, the wizard will check its records and look for a backup that was previously made. Well, its records won't show the backup you did because we wiped the slate clean when we reinstalled Windows from scratch. Selecting this option will give us the opportunity to find where this backup job exists. Once you've selected the option, click "Next."

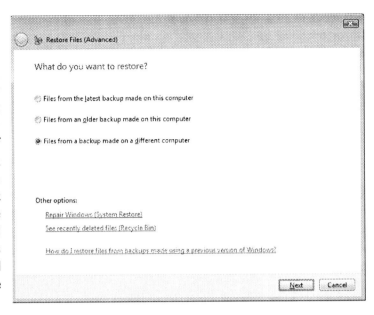

On the "Where is the backup [...]" screen, you can now specify where your backup is located. If your backup is on an external hard drive, you'll want to select the first option and find it in the dropdown list (when plugged in, the Windows operating system refers to these types of drives as "local disks"). If however, your backup is located on a network you have set up (such as on a server share), then you would select the second option and either browse to the location or type in the location in the following format:

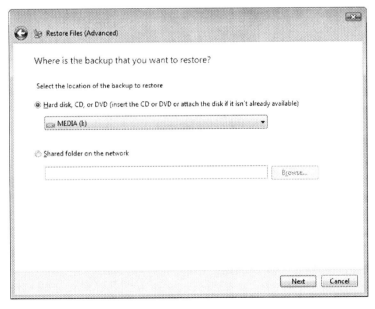

\\ComputerName\ShareName

You'll see in the example, my backup was stored on an external hard drive (the "I" drive). Once you've made your choices, select "Next."

If you put in the correct information on the previous screen, Windows Backup should now present you with a list of backups that it found. Simply select the backup entry with the correct date you would like to restore from and click "Next." In most cases, you'd probably be selecting the backup with the most recent date.

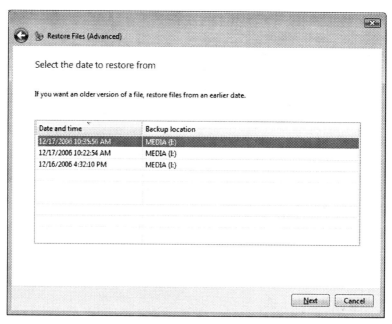

This next screen determines what you will be restoring. This one gets to be a little trickier. You now have some different options... you could go through and find specific files and/or folders of files or you could restore everything that was in the backup.

First off, I'd like to suggest that as long as you have a decent amount of hard drive space on your computer that you should plan on restoring to a single location and then manually moving the files to their proper locations. The reason I point this out is that when you reinstalled the Windows OS, it's very possible that the folder structure may have changed and things may not go into their proper locations - even possibly to the point of screwing up the Windows OS.

That said - my recommendation is that if you've backed up everything on your computer, then you probably don't need to restore all those files because most will probably be system files that are already on the computer - and some might even be problem files that caused you to have to reinstall the Windows operating system in the first place. I would restore most of the files that I discussed as the recommendations to be backed up in "Chapter 18 - What Do I Need to Back Up in the Windows Vista OS?"

One of the first things I would recommend doing is showing hidden files and folders, as well as protected operating system files. You will need to do this if you want to browse to folders such as the ones that hold your cookies. Once you've done the restore, you will want to shut this back off. To show these files, go into "Computer" by clicking on the "Start" button and selecting "Computer." Then click on "Organize" and then "Folder and Search Options."

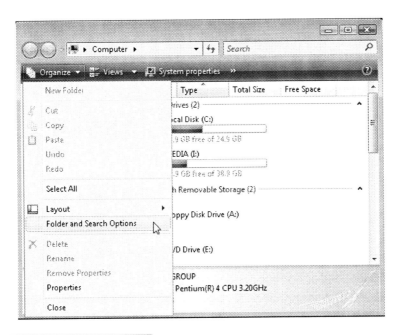

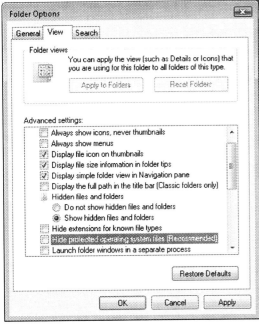

On the "View" tab, look for "Show hidden files and folders," and select it. Then uncheck the box for on "Hide protected operating system files (Recommended)," and click "OK." When prompted with the warning, click "Yes" to apply the changes.

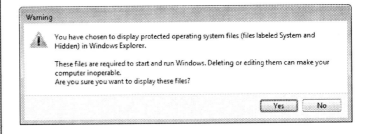

221

Now that that's done, you'll be able to see certain folders like the one that contains your cookies. So, let's get back to our restoration of files. Head back over to the "Restore Files (Advanced)" screen and then click on the "Add folders…" button…

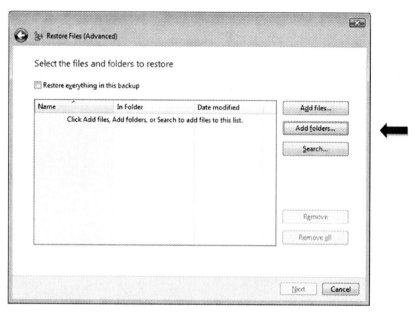

In the "Add folder to restore" screen, you now want to browse to a folder containing items that you will want to restore. Remember that the folders you are looking at are not the ones on your live installation of the Windows OS, but they represent the folder structure that is in your backup that was created.

In the example screenshot, you'll see that I browsed my way through the backup set to "C:\Users\Jim." If you remember from the recommendations of files to back up, a good majority of important files are found in your user directory. So looking at the screenshot, you'll see that within my user directory, I selected "Desktop" and then will click on the "Add" button to add this to the list.

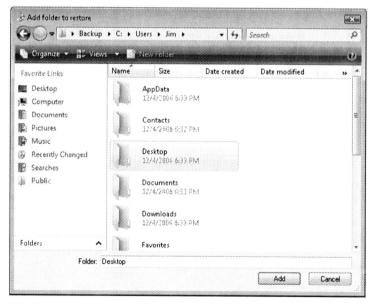

222

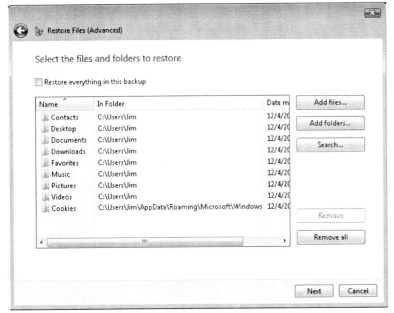

You'll now see that the "Desktop" folder was added to the list of files and folders to be restored.

You now want to click on "Browse folders" again and repeat the process for every folder containing files that you want added to the restore. If you have a specific file that you want restored (and not the entire folder), click on "Browse files" and add that file to the restore.

In this screenshot, you'll see a sample of the folders that I would recommend restoring. These include "Documents," "Favorites," "Pictures," and more. Depending on where you stored information on your computer before you reinstalled the Windows Vista operating system, you may have other folders or different locations to add. Also, if you have other users that were using the computer before, you will probably want to add their folders as well. Once you've added the folders and files that you want to restore, click "Next." Keep in mind that you can always go through this process again and restore more folders and files later if you forgot any!

When prompted for the location to restore the files to, I will say once again that I recommend restoring to a different location and then moving the files to the correct location. To do this, change the option to restore "In the following location" and then click "Browse."

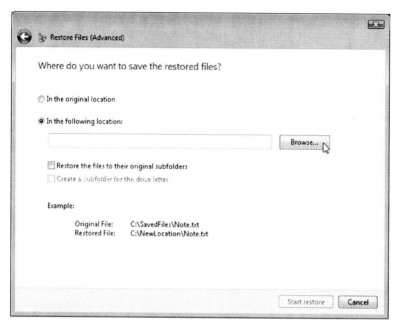

For convenience, I would suggest creating a folder on your desktop to store the files. To do this, browse to your desktop, which should be in "C:\Users\[User Name]\Desktop, and click once on the "Desktop" folder. Then click the "Make New Folder" button.

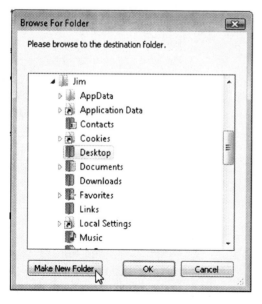 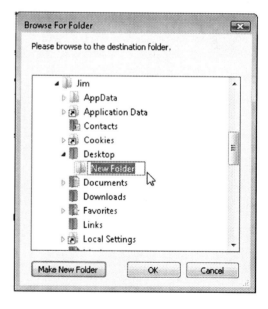

When the folder appears with the text "New Folder" highlighted, type in the name you would like to call the folder, such as "Restored Files" and then press the "Enter" key. Ensure that the folder you created is selected and then click "OK."

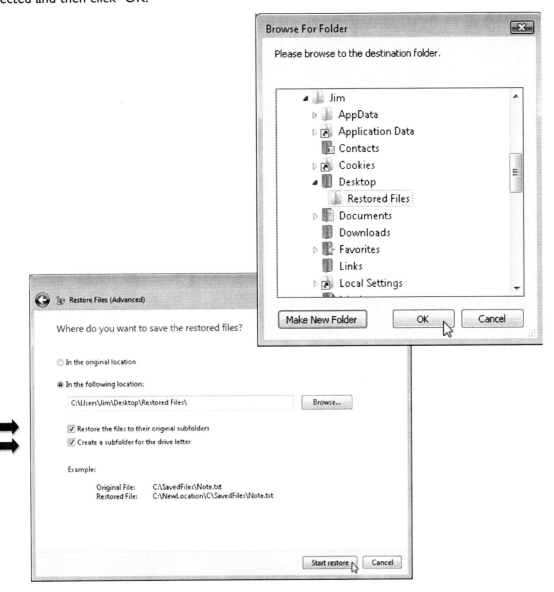

You should now be returned back to the "Where do you want to save the restored files?" screen and the path to your new folder should be showing in the text box. I would also suggest checking the boxes to "Restore the files to their original subfolders" and "Create a subfolder for the drive letter." Once you're ready to go, click on the "Start Restore" button.

The restore process will then begin. Depending on the number and size of the files, the time this takes may vary. You will see a progress bar as the files are being restored to show you... well, to show you the progress.

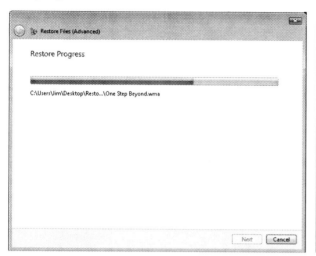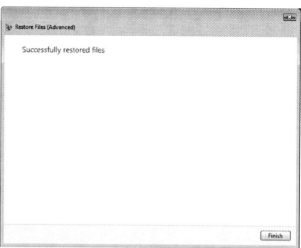

I hope that when everything's been restored, you'll be prompted with a "Successfully restored files" screen. Click "Finish" to exit the "Restore Files (Advanced)" program.

Now we just need to move the data files we restored to their correct locations. First, open up the folder you created on your desktop by double-clicking on it.

Then click on the "Start" button and in the search box, type in **explorer.exe** and press the "Enter" key.

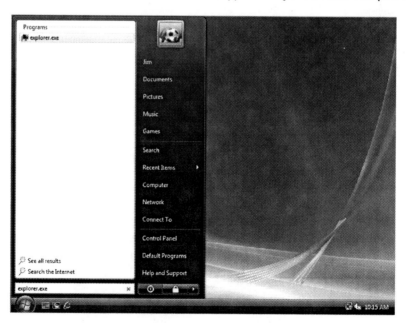

When the window opens, it will likely start you in the "Documents" folder of the user logged in. Using the folders in the left pane, find the "Desktop" folder within your user folder and click on it...

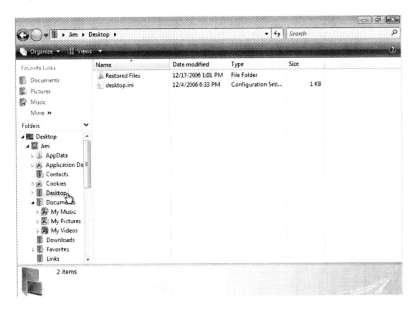

Now, go back to the open window that has the restored files in it ("Restored Files" in my example) and find the "Desktop" folder for your user name. The path along the top will be something like "-> Restored Files -> C -> Users -> [User Name] -> Desktop." Open that folder and let's start.

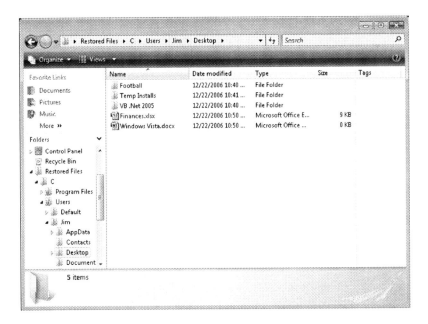

227

Hold down the "Ctrl" key and then press the "a" key. This should highlight all files and folders in this folder. You can let go of the keys if you haven't yet! Now, right-click on one of the highlighted files and select "Cut" from the menu.

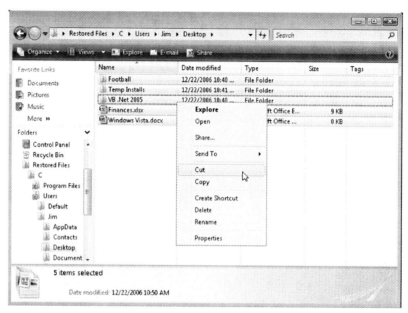

Go back to your other open window that has your live desktop showing. Right-click in an open area of the right pane and select "Paste" from the menu.

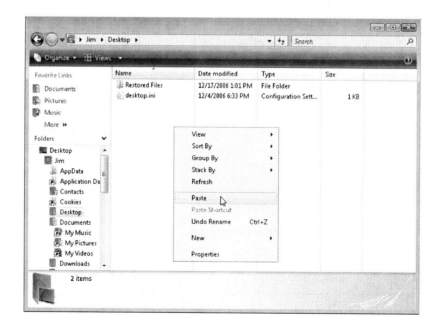

Your files should now be moved to the desktop. If you're logged in as the same user whose desktop files you just moved, you should now be able to minimize the windows and see the files on your actual desktop.

Now you just need to repeat the process for the other folders that you restored. For example, you want to move the contents of the restored "Favorites" folder to the live "Favorites" folder. The same goes for the restored contents of the "Documents" folder to actual "Documents" folder.

Once you have moved all contents to their correct locations, you can delete the "Restored Files" folder from your desktop. You will then want to turn off the ability for the Windows OS to show protected operating system files in order to prevent accidental damage to your computer down the line. Go into "Computer" by click on the "Start" button and selecting "Computer." Then click on "Organize" and then "Folder and Search Options."

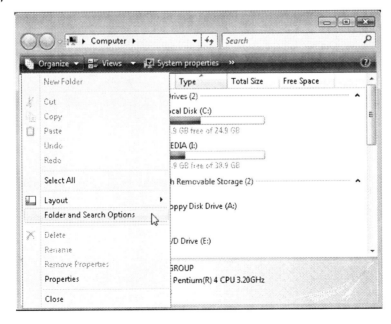

229

On the "View" tab, look for "Show hidden files and folders," and deselect it. Then check the box for on "Hide protected operating system files (Recommended)," and click "OK."

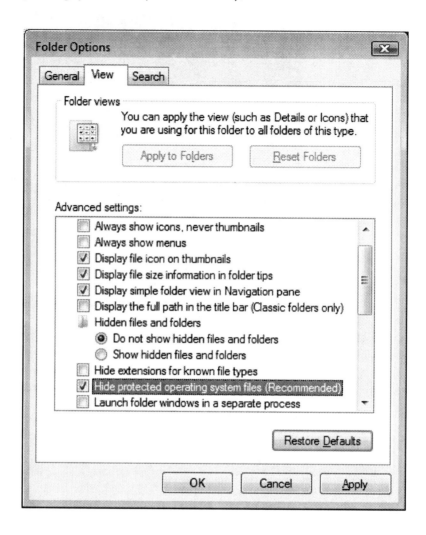

So that's all there is to it! Congratulations on performing a restore of your data back to your computer!

X. The Basics of Migrating to a New Computer

chapter 32

The Basics of Migrating

You finally broke down and decided to get a new computer - you dragged out using the old computer for as long as possible, but couldn't take it anymore. You have some excitement thinking about your new "toy" when you get it through the doorstep. You unpack it, get it all set up, and are ready to go... but hey, wait a minute! Nothing looks even close to the way you like it! You spent years getting your settings just the way you wanted them! Oh, yeah, and how are you going to get all your data from your old computer to your new computer?!

Well, you've come to the right section. I want to help you get things from your old computer to your new computer in the least painful way possible. My assumption is that if you're buying a new computer, it will be computer with the Windows Vista operating system. And fortunately, with the Windows Vista OS, Microsoft provides an easy and straightforward tool to be able to transfer your files and settings - "Windows Easy Transfer."

I've purposely made this the last section because I wanted to make sure you had a good understanding of how Windows operating system stores your user profiles, settings, data, etc. before moving onto the fun stuff. Understanding the "how it works" can sometimes make the actual doing of things a lot easier on you.

In the next couple of chapters, I'll show you how to migrate your files and settings from the Windows 2000, Windows XP, or Windows Vista operating systems to a new computer running the Windows Vista OS. You have a few options on how to do this...

233

The first method is the simplest - it involves using what's generally referred to as an "USB easy transfer cable." This is a cable that's meant to connect two computers together through a USB port on each computer. They usually run about $25 to $50 and can be purchased online or at electronics stores like Best Buy or Circuit City. You connect one end to each computer and then run the "Windows Easy Transfer" software and live happily ever after.

The second method is not very difficult - it just requires an extra step. It involves using a temporary storage location. If you've been following my recommendations throughout the book, you may already have an external USB hard drive that you're using for your backups. As long as you have enough free space on the drive, you can use that. In this scenario, you will perform a two-step process - you save out your data and settings from your old computer onto the external hard drive using "Windows Easy Transfer" and then you use the drive to import your data and settings to your new computer using the "Windows Easy Transfer" program. Not as easy as using the "USB easy transfer cable," but if you already have an external USB hard drive, it can save you about $50.

Other methods include using network connectivity between the two computers or using other removable media such as a USB flash drive, CDs, or DVDs. However, we will concentrate on the first two methods in the next chapters. It's important to note that the "Windows Easy Transfer" program only supports migrations from the Windows 2000, Windows XP, or Windows Vista operating systems and only to the Windows Vista operating system. If you have an older operating system you are trying to move your data and settings from, such as Windows 98 or Windows Me, this tool will not work for you. In that case, you will likely need to recreate your settings, but can bring over your data by either backing it up or copying it to an external hard drive and then copying or restoring the data from the drive to your new computer. If you do this, please manually copy data carefully to each location since the paths will probably not match. For instance, your desktop items in in the Windows 98 OS are found in "C:\WINDOWS\Desktop." However, in the Windows Vista OS, the path to your desktop items can vary with each user and follows a structure similar to "C:\Users\[User Name]\Desktop."

Please note that if you're migrating from the Windows 2000 OS, you can use "Windows Easy Transfer" to transfer files to a computer running the Windows Vista operating system, but you cannot transfer system and program settings.

If you're migrating from the Windows 2000, Windows XP, or Windows Vista OS to a computer running the Windows Vista OS, read on to see how easy it is to move from your old computer to your new computer! More information can also be found in the Microsoft article "How to use Windows Easy Transfer to migrate files and settings from one Windows-based computer to a nother Windows Vista-based computer," currently found at:
http://support.microsoft.com/kb/928634.

234

chapter 33

Migrating to the Windows Vista OS Using an External USB Hard Drive

As you read in "Chapter 32 - The Basics of Migrating," migrating your data and settings from an older computer running the Windows 2000, Windows XP, or Windows Vista OS to a new computer running the Windows Vista OS, can be fairly painless. This is particularly true if you have an "USB easy transfer cable." For this to work, both computers must have at least one USB port on them. My suggestion is to read this chapter, as well as the next to determine which of these methods suits you best. If the process in the next chapter makes more sense for you to use to keep things simple, then you may want to order one of these cables.

If however you don't want to get one of these cables, you can use an external USB hard drive... just make sure it has enough free space on it to be able to fit your data and settings.

First, you will need to make sure that you install all programs on your new computer before continuing. Using the "Windows Easy Transfer" program, you will be able to migrate the settings for the applications, but not the application itself. It is important that the applications be installed first so the settings can be properly applied. Installing a program after you've already performed the migration will likely just let the program overwrite your personal settings you've imported in with its own default installation settings. As a reminder, keep in mind that if your old computer is running the Windows 2000 operating system, you cannot transfer application settings anyway - only data.

Using the USB hard drive is a two to three step process to go through, depending on what operating system your old computer is running.

If you're running the Windows 2000 or Windows XP OS on your old computer, the steps we'll need to take are this:
1. Install the "Windows Easy Transfer" software on your old computer.
2. Save all settings and data from your old computer onto your USB hard drive.
3. Import all settings from your USB hard drive into your new computer running the Windows Vista OS.

If you're running the Windows Vista OS on your old computer, you'll follow the same steps, except you get the bonus of skipping the first step... go ahead and skip ahead to Step 2. Let's get started...

Step 1 - Install the "Windows Easy Transfer" software on your old computer (this is only if your old computer is running the Windows 2000 or Windows XP OS).

There are a couple different ways to get the "Windows Easy Transfer" software onto your old computer. One way to do this is by running the "Windows Easy Transfer" program on your new computer running the Windows Vista OS, following the prompts, and using a USB hard drive to transfer the data. This is effective, but time-consuming. The method I am going to show you is straightforward - we're just going to download and install the program on the old computer.

Get on your old computer and open up the Internet Explorer browser. "Windows Easy Transfer for Windows XP and Windows 2000" can currently be found at **http://www.microsoft.com/downloads/ details.aspx?FamilyId=2B6F1631-973A-45C7-A4EC-4928FA173266&displaylang=en.** Option 1 is to type that in (not so much fun!). Option 2 is to type "Windows Easy Transfer for Windows XP and Windows 2000" into a search engine like Google web search **(http://www.google.com)**. The first link (or close to it) should be the same as the long one you're trying to avoid typing. Either way should take you to a page to download the "Windows Easy Transfer" program. You will want to follow the directions from there - probably needing to click on the "Continue" button, and then downloading the correct file. The file "tfrcable_x86.exe" is likely the one you want. This is for 32-bit systems, which is probably what your old computer is running. If you know you're running a 64-bit system (not very common for the typical home user), you would download the other "tfrcable_x64.exe" file. Download the file and save it to a location, such as your desktop.

Once you've downloaded the file, you will want to run it. Go to the location you downloaded it to launch it. Once the file extracts and takes you to the wizard, click "Next" to continue.

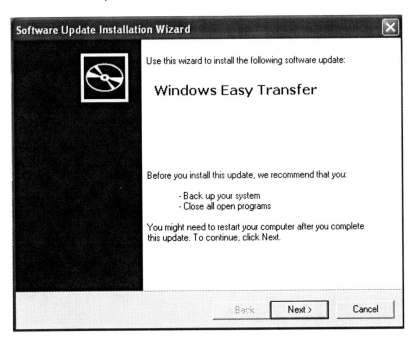

On the License Agreement screen, feel free to read it if you want and then select "I Agree" and click the "Next" button.

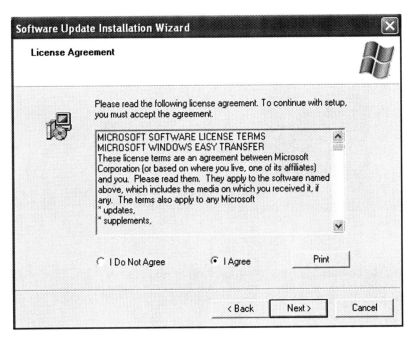

The software will then install...

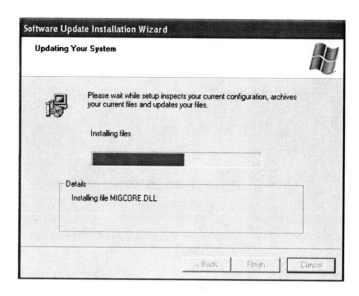

Once the install is complete, click on "Finish."

Mission accomplished. You're now ready to start the migration process. **Let the fun begin!**

Step 2 - Save all settings and data from your old computer onto your USB hard drive

Connect the USB drive to your old computer and make sure that it's powered on. You now need to start the "Windows Easy Transfer" program.

In the Windows 2000 or Windows XP OS, you can start the program by clicking on the "Start" button, going to "Programs" or "All Programs" (depending on how your "Start" menu is set up), and selecting "Windows Easy Transfer."

If you're running the Windows Vista OS on your old computer, you can start the program by clicking on the "Start" button, going to "Programs" or "All Programs" (depending on how your "Start" menu is set up), then "Accessories," "System Tools," and finally selecting "Windows Easy Transfer."

Either way, once the application comes up, click "Next" to continue.

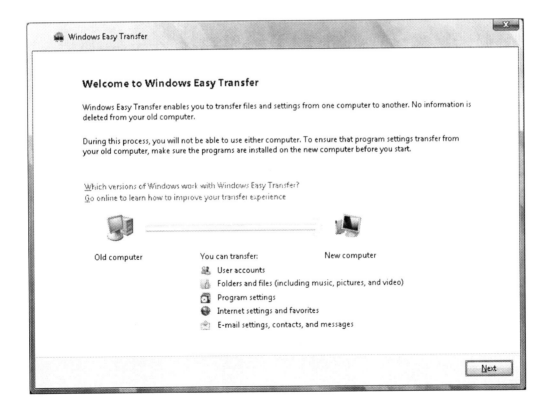

If any programs are still open on the computer, the "Windows Easy Transfer" will let you know. You can click "Close all" to have the programs closed automatically. If you need to get to a program to close it yourself (maybe because you need to save it first), you can hold down the "Ctrl" key and then press the "Esc" key. This will open the "Start" menu, and show you the taskbar so you can click on a program and close it yourself. Once all programs are closed (or you've clicked the "Close all" button), the program will automatically move to the next screen.

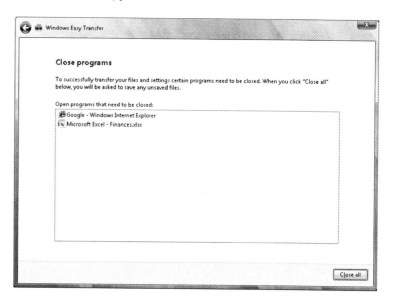

If you're running the Windows 2000 or Windows XP OS on your old computer, you can skip the next couple of screens. If your old computer is running the Windows Vista operating system, however, you get a couple extra screens you have to answer. On the dialog asking if you want to start a new transfer or continue an existing transfer, click on "Start a new transfer." Then when asked which computer you're using, let "Windows Easy Transfer" know that you are on the source computer by clicking "My old computer."

OK, now everyone should be back on the same page, whether your old computer is running the Windows 2000, Windows XP, or Windows Vista operating system. At this point, "Windows Easy Transfer" needs to find out *how* you want to transfer files and settings. On this screen, you want to select "Use a CD, DVD, or other removable media" - this will be your USB drive.

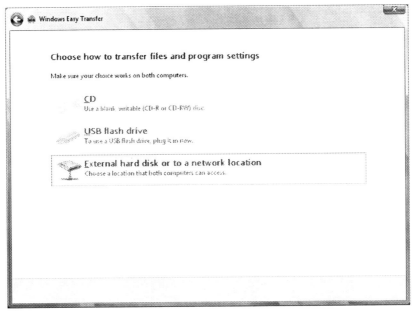

Now go ahead and select "External hard disk [...]".

You're now asked where you want to save your files and settings to. This is when you want to browse to a location on your USB hard drive. Your files and settings are all put into a single file (ending in ".MIG"), so it isn't critical that they be put into a separate folder. However, in my example, you'll see I'll be saving everything in a file called "SaveData.MIG" in a folder named "from_old_computer" on my USB drive. For security, you can also add a password to the file, but that's optional.

Once you have the information you need entered on this screen, click "Next to continue."

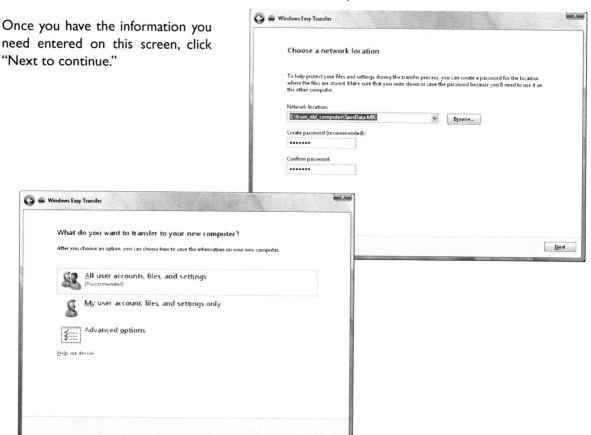

Now you need to decide what to transfer. In most cases, you'll probably want to transfer everything - "All user accounts, files, and settings." However, if you have several user accounts on the computer that are never used, you may want to select the option for "My user account, files, and settings" only. Keep in mind, however, that means only the account of the user logged in will have his/her account and files migrated. All other files and settings for other users on the computer (such as their "Documents," desktop items, etc.) will not be saved out to be imported into your new computer. The last choice for "Advanced options" should only be used if you are an advanced user and have specific choices you want to examine. Again, in most cases, you'll want to select the option for "All user accounts, files, and settings."

After you selected what you wanted to transfer, "Windows Easy Transfer" will immediately go to work on finding out about how much data needs to be transferred to your USB drive. You can skip this by clicking "Next," but unless you're in a big hurry and know you have plenty of space on your USB drive, I would just let it run.

You're now shown a screen of what will be transferred for you. If you don't see everything you want, you can click on "Customize" to add other files or folders. Otherwise, click "Transfer" to let the ball start rolling. As a side note, don't compare the size of the data you have to transfer to what you see here - mine is on a test computer and doesn't have very much data on it.

Your files and settings now start the transfer to your USB drive...

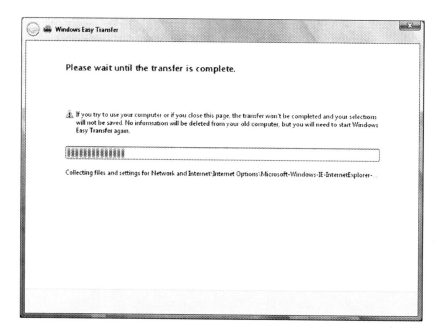

"Windows Easy Transfer" will let you know when it's done transferring everything to your USB drive. You're almost done... onto step 3!

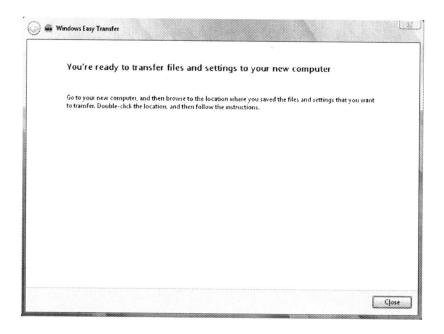

Step 3 - Import all settings from your USB hard drive
into your new computer running the Windows Vista OS

If you haven't already done so, disconnect your USB hard drive from your old computer by first clicking on the "Safely Remove Hardware" icon in the notification area by the clock to remove it from the system and then disconnecting it from the old computer.

Connect the USB hard drive to your new computer running the Windows Vista OS and make sure it's powered on. Then close any documents or programs that you may be working in.

If you are an administrator, you can launch the "Windows Easy Transfer" program by clicking on the "Start" button, going to "Programs" or "All Programs" (depending on how your "Start" menu is set up), then "Accessories," "System Tools," and finally selecting "Windows Easy Transfer." If prompted for permission, click "Continue."

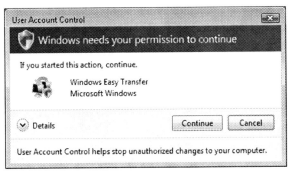

If you are not an administrator, you can launch the "Windows Easy Transfer" program by clicking on the "Start" button, going to "Programs" or "All Programs" (depending on how your "Start" menu is set up), then "Accessories," and "System Tools." Then right-click on the "Windows Easy Transfer" shortcut and select "Run as administrator." Enter in the password for an administrator account and click "OK" to continue.

When "Windows Easy Transfer" comes up, click "Next" to continue.

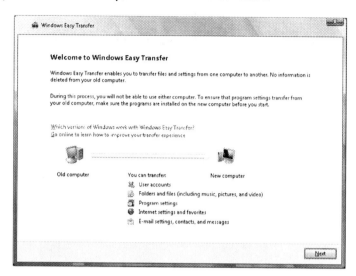

If any programs are still open on the computer, the "Windows Easy Transfer" will let you know. You can click "Close all" to have the programs closed automatically. If you need to get to an application to close it yourself (maybe because you need to save it first), you can hold down the "Ctrl" key and then press the "Esc" key. This will open the "Start" menu, and show you the taskbar so you can click on a program and close it yourself. Once all programs are closed (or you've clicked the "Close all" button), the program will automatically move to the next screen.

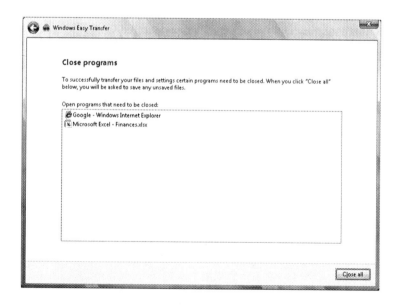

On the dialog asking if you want to start a new transfer or continue an existing transfer, click on "Continue a transfer in progress."

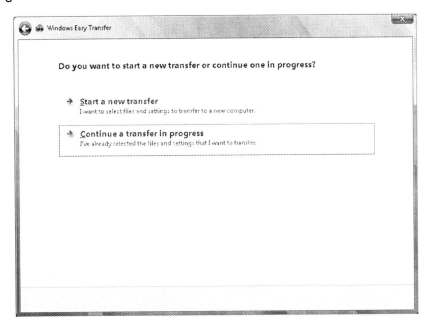

When asked if your computers are connected on a network, select "No, I've copied files and settings to a CD, DVD, or other removable media."

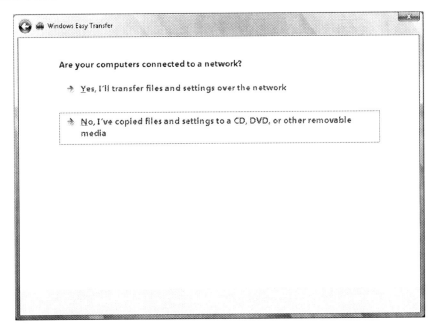

When asked where you saved your files and settings, choose "On an external hard disk or network location."

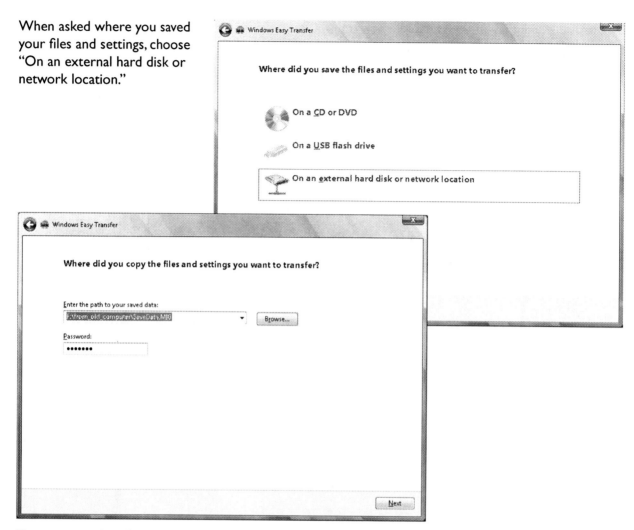

You now need to let "Windows Easy Transfer" know where you copied your files and settings. Click the browse button to locate the location. If you set a password in the last step when creating your transferred data, you'll need to put one in here. By the way, if you noticed, when I created my data transfer file in the last step, the path was "X:\from_old_computer[...]," but now it's "F:\ from_old_computer [...]." Why is it a different drive letter? By default, the Windows operating system assigns USB devices the next available drive letter. On my old computer, I had set the drive letter to be "X" using the "Disk Management" console (click on the "Start" button, then "Run," type in diskmgmt.msc and click "OK"). However, on the new computer, I have a "C" and "D" partition and a CD drive with the letter of "E," so the Windows OS just gave it the next drive letter available on my computer - "F."

Once you've made your selections on the "Where did you copy the files and settings you want to transfer" screen, click "Next."

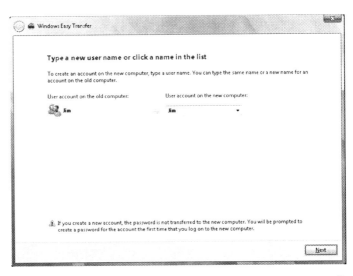

On this screen, you now have an opportunity to match user accounts from the old computer to the new computer. This will let "Windows Easy Transfer" know whom the source and destination users are to properly transfer files and settings. You may have an account named "Robert" on the left column and one on the right named "Bob." Just make sure to match them up as you want them using the dropdown box. If you had more than one user account on your old computer, but have not created those accounts in the Windows Vista OS, this is an opportunity to type in a name on the right to have it automatically created using the settings and files from the account on the left. Once you've got everything set correctly, click "Next."

If you are dealing with more than one partition, you will see this next screen. It gives you an opportunity to determine which drives go to what. So if your old computer had a "C" and a "D" drive for instance, and your new computer has only a "C" drive, files on the "D" drive would need to go onto the "C" drive. Make any changes as necessary and then click "Next" to go on.

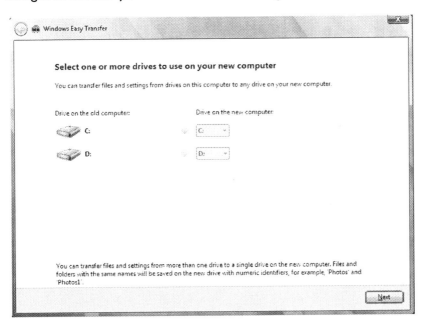

You're now shown the list of files to be transferred - click "Transfer" and the migration will start.

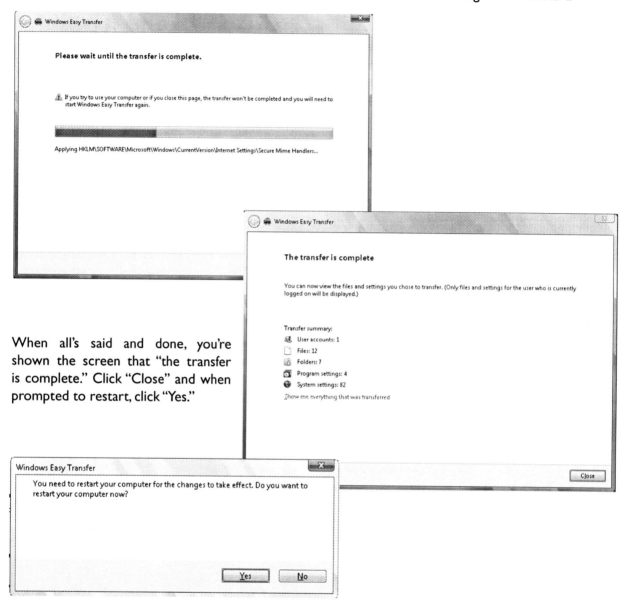

When all's said and done, you're shown the screen that "the transfer is complete." Click "Close" and when prompted to restart, click "Yes."

You're done... congratulations! That wasn't so bad was it? Once your computer finishes restarting, you should be presented with all users that were transferred and upon logging in, your old settings and data should now be there for you. Now aren't you glad you got this book?

250

chapter 34

Migrating to the Windows Vista OS Using an "Easy Transfer USB Cable"

As you read in "Chapter 32 - The Basics of Migrating," migrating your data and settings from an older computer running the Windows 2000, Windows XP, or Windows Vista OS to a new computer running the Windows Vista OS can be fairly painless. This is particularly true if you have an "USB Easy Transfer cable." For this to work, both computers must have at least one USB port on them.

Keep in mind that the cables currently run about $25 to $50 and can be found through the eBay website or one of the many shopping portals. By going to the Yahoo! Shopping (**http://shopping.ya-hoo.com**) website or Froogle™ product search (**http://froogle.google.com**) and typing in the phrase "Windows Easy Transfer" (with the quotes), along with the words "USB" and "cable" (without the quotes), you'll find results from which you can find a reputable store. You may want to sort your results by price so you don't see the "sponsored results" first.

First, you will need to make sure that you install all programs on your new computer before continuing. Using the "Windows Easy Transfer" program, you will be able to migrate the settings for the applications, but not the application itself. Therefore, it is important that the applications be installed first so the settings can be properly applied. Installing a program after you've already performed the migration will likely just let the program overwrite your personal settings you've imported in with its own default installation settings. As a reminder, keep in mind that if your old computer is running the Windows 2000 operating system, you cannot transfer application settings anyway - only data.

Once you have your cable and have installed all applications on your new computer, there is a two to three step process to go through, depending on what operating system your old computer is running.

If you're running the Windows 2000 or Windows XP OS on your old computer, the steps we'll need to take are this:
1. Install the "Windows Easy Transfer" software on your old computer.
2. Connect both computers using the "USB Easy Transfer cable."
3. Transfer all files and settings to your new computer running the Windows Vista OS.

If you're running the Windows Vista OS on your old computer, you'll follow the same steps, except you get the bonus of skipping the first step... go ahead and skip ahead to Step 2. Let's get started ...

Step 1 - Install the "Windows Easy Transfer" software on your old computer (this is only if your old computer is running the Windows 2000 or Windows XP OS).

Your USB Easy Transfer cable should have come with a CD that has the "Windows Easy Transfer" software as well as any software drivers for the cable on it. Pop it into the CD tray of your old computer and follow the manufacturer's instructions to install the software. That's all there is to it and you can skip ahead to Step 2.

If it did not come with the "Windows Easy Transfer" software, there are a couple different ways to get the software onto your old computer. One way to do this is by running the "Windows Easy Transfer" program on your new computer running th Windows Vista OS, following the prompts, and using a USB hard drive or flash drive to transfer the data. This is effective, but time-consuming. The method I am going to show you is straightforward - we're just going to download and install the program on the old computer.

Get on your old computer and open up the Internet Explorer browser. "Windows Easy Transfer for Windows XP and Windows 2000" can currently be found at **http://www.microsoft.com/downloads/ details.aspx?FamilyId=2B6F1631-973A-45C7-A4EC-4928FA173266&displaylang=en.** Option 1 is to type that in (not so much fun!). Option 2 is to type "Windows Easy Transfer for Windows XP and Windows 2000" into a search engine like Google web search (**http://www.google.com**). The first link (or close to it) should be the same as the long one you're trying to avoid typing. Either way should take you to a page to download the "Windows Easy Transfer" program. You will want to follow the directions from there - probably needing to click on the "Continue" button, and then downloading the correct file. The file "tfrcable_x86.exe" is likely the one you want. This is for 32-bit systems, which is probably what your old computer is running. If you know you're running a 64-bit system (not very common for the typical home user), you would download the other "tfrcable_x64.exe" file. Download the file and save it to a location, such as your desktop.

Chapter 34 – Migrating to the Windows Vista OS Using an "Easy Transfer USB Cable"

Once you've downloaded the file, you will want to run it. Go to the location you downloaded it to launch it. Once the file extracts and takes you to the wizard, click "Next" to continue.

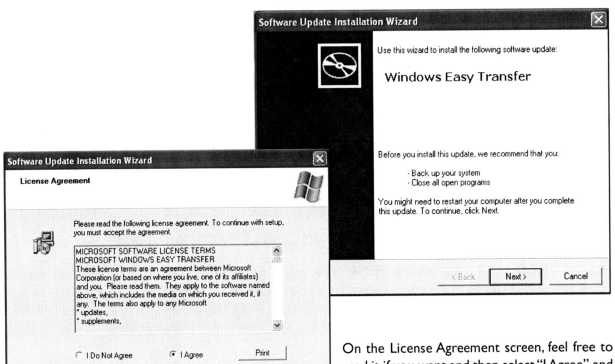

On the License Agreement screen, feel free to read it if you want and then select "I Agree" and click the "Next" button.

The software will then install...

Once the install is complete, click on "Finish."

Mission accomplished. You're now
ready to start the migration process.

Let the fun begin!

Step 2 - Connect both computers using the "USB Easy Transfer cable"

Connect the cable to the old computer, following any special manufacturer's instructions. Then connect the other end of the cable to your new computer. How was that for straightforward?

Step 3 - Transfer all files and settings to your new computer running the Windows Vista OS

The "Windows Easy Transfer" program should automatically launch once the computers are connected.

If the "Windows Easy Transfer" program does not automatically start and you are an administrator, you can launch the program by clicking on the "Start" button, going to "Programs" or "All Programs" (depending on how your "Start" menu is set up), then "Accessories," "System Tools," and finally selecting "Windows Easy Transfer." If prompted for permission, click "Continue."

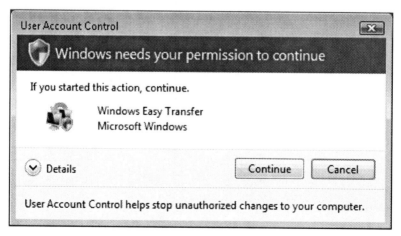

If the "Windows Easy Transfer" program does not automatically start and you are not an administrator, you can launch the program by clicking on the "Start" button, going to "Programs" or "All Programs" (depending on how your "Start" menu is set up), then "Accessories," and "System Tools." Then right-click on the "Windows Easy Transfer" shortcut and select "Run as administrator." Enter in the password for an administrator account.

I don't have screenshots to provide you with for the next couple of things that take place because as of this writing, the "USB Easy Transfer cables" are not readily available. It's also possible that some of my instructions will not necessarily come in the precise order. However, it should be very straightforward and all the pertinent information should be here. Here is what will likely take place...

You should get to a point where you are asked to specify what to transfer. In most cases, you'll probably want to transfer everything - "All user accounts, files, and settings." However, if you have several user accounts on the computer that are never used, you may want to select the option for "My user account, files, and settings" only. Keep in mind, however, that means only the account of the user logged in will have his/her account and files migrated. All other files and settings for other users on the computer (such as their "Documents," desktop items, etc.) will not be saved out to be imported into your new computer. The last choice for "Advanced options" should only be used if you are an advanced user and have specific choices you want to examine. Again, in most cases, you'll want to select the option for "All user accounts, files, and settings."

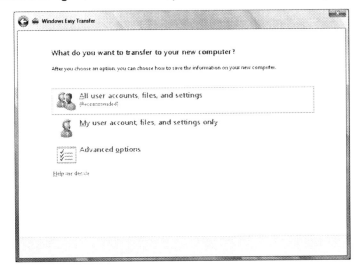

After you selected what you wanted to transfer, "Windows Easy Transfer" will probably immediately go to work on finding out about how much data will be transferred. You can skip this by clicking "Next," but unless you're in a big hurry, I would just let it run.

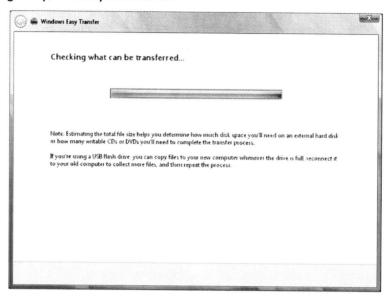

You will likely be shown a screen of what will be transferred for you. If you don't see everything you want, you can click on "Customize" to add other files or folders. Otherwise, click "Transfer" to let the ball start rolling. As a side note, don't compare the size of the data you have to transfer to what you see here - mine is on a test computer and doesn't have very much data on it.

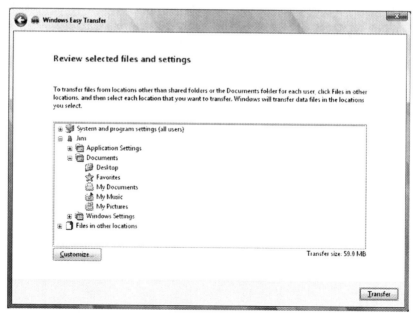

Another screen should give you an opportunity to match user accounts from the old computer to the new computer. This will let "Windows Easy Transfer" know whom the source and destination users are to properly transfer files and settings. You may have an account named "Robert" on the left column and one on the right named "Bob." Just make sure to match them up as you want them using the dropdown box. If you had more than one user account on your old computer, but have not created those accounts in the Windows Vista OS, this is an opportunity to type in a name on the right to have it automatically created using the settings and files from the account on the left. Once you've got everything set correctly, click "Next."

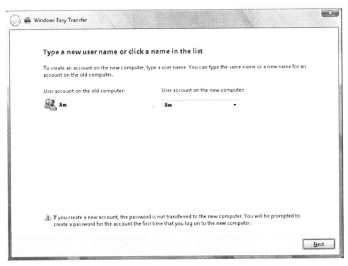

If you are dealing with more than one partition, you will see this next screen. It gives you an opportunity to determine which drives go to what. So if your old computer had a "C" and a "D" drive for instance, and your new computer has only a "C" drive, files on the "D" drive would need to go onto the "C" drive. Make any changes as necessary and then click "Next" to go on.

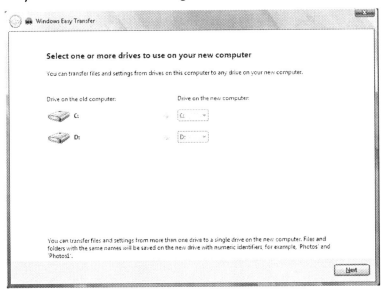

You should then be shown the list of files to be transferred - click "Transfer" and the migration will start.

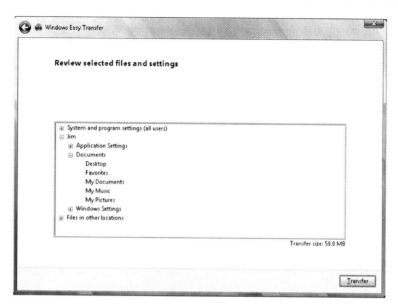

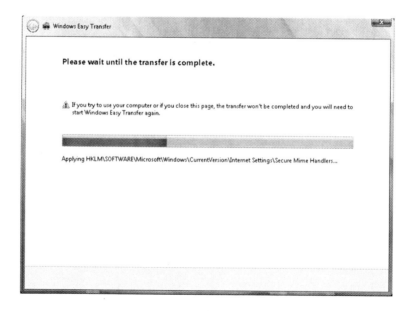

When all's said and done, you're shown the screen that "the transfer is complete." Click "Close" and when prompted to restart the new computer, click "Yes."

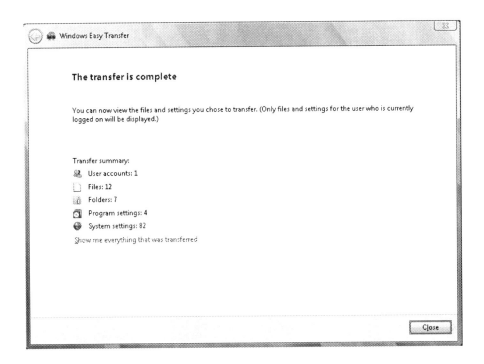

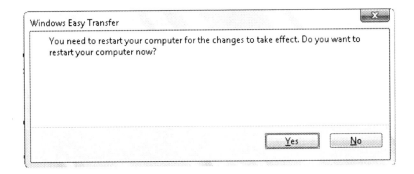

You're done... congratulations! That wasn't so bad was it? Once your computer finishes restarting, you should be presented with all users that were transferred and upon logging in, your old settings and data should now be there for you. Technology at its best!

Conclusion

We've come to the end of the book. We've covered some of the most important parts of buying a new computer, as well as protecting and maintaining it. I hope that you've taken some of the information you've learned and already begun to implement it.

There's no way one book can teach you all there is to know about maintaining your computer, but if you've taken your time and understand what you've read throughout this book, you should now have a good foundation and can continue to build on that knowledge. This is important, because things will change - new types of threats will emerge and the methods to protect your computer will evolve. Because of this, you will need to continue to expand on what you know in order to ensure that your computer, and more importantly, your data, is protected.

Remember, if you run into a problem or something you can't figure out with your computer, someone else has likely run into the same problem. And the best part is that someone has likely documented that information on a website somewhere on the Internet. Use the Google or Yahoo! search engine and type in all or part of that error message or the task you're trying to accomplish... you'll probably get back enough results to point you in the right direction. The Internet is like a library at your fingertips - just remember that not all people are do-gooders. So, unless the information is from a reputable business like Microsoft, for instance, just use the information as a pointer to get you started to make a more informed decision on what to do next.

Thanks for taking the time to read this book. I hope it's helped you gain a better understanding of computers and the importance of protecting them. Good luck in all your future endeavors.

– Jim

Q

R

Index

Printed in the United Kingdom
by Lightning Source UK Ltd.
136542UK00001B/194/A